COMPACT *Research*

Drunk Driving

Current Issues

ReferencePoint Press®

San Diego, CA

Other books in the Compact Research series include:

Drunk Driving

by Peggy J. Parks

Current Issues

ReferencePoint Press®

San Diego, CA

For more information, contact:
ReferencePoint Press, Inc.
PO Box 27779
San Diego, CA 92198
www. ReferencePointPress.com

Picture credits:
Maury Aaseng: 33–35, 47–49, 61–63, 75–77
AP Images: 15, 17

LIBRARY OF CONGRESS CATALOGING-IN-PUBLICATION DATA

Parks, Peggy J., 1951–
    Drunk driving / by Peggy J Parks.
        p. cm.—(Compact research series)
    Includes bibliographical references and index.
    ISBN-13: 978-1-60152-072-2 (hardback)
    ISBN-10: 1-60152-072-7 (hardback)
    1. Drunk driving—United States. I. Title.
    HE5620.D7P364 2008
    363.12'5—dc22

                                                                        2008048499

Contents

Foreword

As modern civilization continues to evolve, its ability to create, store, distribute, and access information expands exponentially. The explosion of information from all media continues to increase at a phenomenal rate. By 2020 some experts predict the worldwide information base will double every 73 days. While access to diverse sources of information and perspectives is paramount to any democratic society, information alone cannot help people gain knowledge and understanding. Information must be organized and presented clearly and succinctly in order to be understood. The challenge in the digital age becomes not the creation of information, but how best to sort, organize, enhance, and present information.

ReferencePoint Press developed the *Compact Research* series with this challenge of the information age in mind. More than any other subject area today, researching current issues can yield vast, diverse, and unqualified information that can be intimidating and overwhelming for even the most advanced and motivated researcher. The *Compact Research* series offers a compact, relevant, intelligent, and conveniently organized collection of information covering a variety of current topics ranging from illegal immigration and deforestation to diseases such as anorexia and meningitis.

The series focuses on three types of information: objective single-author narratives, opinion-based primary source quotations, and facts and statistics. The clearly written objective narratives provide context and reliable background information. Primary source quotes are carefully selected and cited, exposing the reader to differing points of view. And facts and statistics sections aid the reader in evaluating perspectives. Presenting these key types of information creates a richer, more balanced learning experience.

For better understanding and convenience, the series enhances information by organizing it into narrower topics and adding design features that make it easy for a reader to identify desired content. For example, in *Compact Research: Illegal Immigration*, a chapter covering the economic impact of illegal immigration has an objective narrative explaining the various ways the economy is impacted, a balanced section of numerous primary source quotes on the topic, followed by facts and full-color illustrations to encourage evaluation of contrasting perspectives.

The ancient Roman philosopher Lucius Annaeus Seneca wrote, "It is quality rather than quantity that matters." More than just a collection of content, the *Compact Research* series is simply committed to creating, finding, organizing, and presenting the most relevant and appropriate amount of information on a current topic in a user-friendly style that invites, intrigues, and fosters understanding.

Drunk Driving at a Glance

Blood-Alcohol Concentration

Whether someone is intoxicated is determined by a test that measures blood-alcohol concentration (BAC). A BAC of .03 percent means that 100 milliliters of the person's blood contained .03 percent of alcohol. In all states and the District of Columbia, the legal BAC limit is .08 percent.

Drunk Driving Statistics

The National Highway Traffic Safety Administration (NHTSA) reports that in 2007 more than 41,000 people in the United States were killed in traffic crashes, with 12,998 of the deaths resulting from at least one driver who was drunk.

The "Typical" Drunk Driver

People of both sexes, all races and religions, all income levels, and all ages have been arrested for drunk driving. The most common drunk drivers are males aged 21 to 34.

Repeat Offenders

Safety officials say that anywhere from one-third to three-fourths of drunk drivers are repeat offenders who have been charged with at least one previous drunk driving arrest.

Teenagers Driving Drunk

Motor vehicle crashes are the number one cause of death for teenagers. In 2006, 31 percent of teen drivers who were killed had been drinking, and 77 percent of those drivers were not restrained with seat belts.

Laws and Punishment

Some states have much tougher drunk driving laws than others. Some with the harshest penalties are Arizona, Utah, Oregon, and New Mexico, while legislation in South Carolina and North Dakota is much more lenient.

Efforts to Stop Drunk Driving

Law enforcement and traffic safety officials say drunk driving traffic deaths have declined since the 1980s. They attribute the drop to tougher laws, harsher punishments, the minimum drinking age of 21, education programs for teens, and the power of organizations such as Mothers Against Drunk Driving (MADD).

Overview

Some people are just too addicted, too reckless, too destructive, too careless to think about the consequences. Every day, they're out there, plying the roads and in no shape to drive.99

—Laura Sperling, a Florida writer whose father was killed by a drunk driver in 1996.

66**There are few tragedies that bring as much pain to families and communities as these violent crimes caused by drunk drivers.**99

—Ted Poe, Republican congressman from Texas.

On February 22, 2002, Nicole LaFreniere made a mistake that will haunt her for the rest of her life. She had just gotten a new job as a stylist at a Livermore, California, hair salon and she felt like celebrating. She drove to T.G.I. Friday's where she drank a vodka tonic, followed by an even stronger cocktail, and then she and some friends left to visit several other bars. LaFreniere continued to drink alcohol throughout the night. After the bars closed at 2:00 A.M., the group decided to continue partying at the home of a friend. LaFreniere got behind the wheel of her Camaro, her best friend Kyle Alexander and 4 others squeezed in back, and a fifth passenger climbed in the front. On a 2-lane street, LaFreniere was driving about 60 miles per hour (97kph) when she turned a corner and lost control of her car. The Camaro veered sharply to the right, spun around, and continued spinning as it jumped the sidewalk and smashed into a tree. When emergency rescue workers arrived, they saw that the car had been ripped nearly in half, its frame twisted like a pretzel. Three people in the back were dead, including Alexander, and the other 2 passengers were seriously injured. LaFreniere was still strapped in her seat belt when paramedics found her semiconscious and slumped over the bent, broken steering wheel with glass embedded in her head. She suffered internal bleeding, a lacerated liver and spleen, a punctured colon, and back fractures—but those injuries paled in comparison to the devastation and guilt she felt upon learning that her actions had killed 3 people. She explains: "The physical pain was excruciating, but the thought of what I'd done was worse. The deaths of my friends weighed

> " When emergency rescue workers arrived, they saw that the car had been ripped nearly in half, its frame twisted like a pretzel. "

heavily on my mind. . . . I kept wondering, *Why did I survive?*" LaFreniere could not remember anything about the accident, which made it even harder for her to comprehend. "I had all these questions that I couldn't answer," she writes. "*Why didn't I call a cab? Why didn't I make a different choice? Why didn't anyone take my keys away from me?* I did a lot of crying."[1]

At her court hearing, LaFreniere sobbed as she begged the victims' families for forgiveness. She was sentenced to six years in prison, and in December 2005 she was released on parole. Pam Stangland, whose son was killed in the crash, expressed her thoughts after LeFreniere was paroled: "Hopefully, she has changed and can relate a message to others to prevent drunk driving, and doesn't try to make everybody feel sorry for her. . . . She needs to forgive herself and God needs to forgive her, but I can't forgive her."[2]

How Serious a Problem Is Drunk Driving?

When people talk about motor vehicle collisions, they often refer to them as accidents—but according to the National Highway Traffic Safety Administration (NHTSA), the word "accident" has no place in a discussion about drunk driving: "Why do we say 'crash' versus 'accident'? Impaired driving is no 'accident,' it is preventable—a violent crime that kills."[3] NHTSA reports show that during 2007 more than 41,000 people in the United States were killed in traffic crashes, including motorists, pedestrians, and bicyclists, and another 2.5 million were injured. Nearly 13,000 of the deaths resulted from crashes in which a driver of a car or motorcycle was impaired by alcohol. Although the number of alcohol-impaired fatalities has declined since the 1980s, drunk driving remains a serious problem.

Alcohol and Recreational Vehicles: A Deadly Combination

Drunk driving laws in the United States apply not only to cars and trucks, but also to recreational vehicles. Studies have shown that many people who would not get behind the wheel of a car when they are drunk often think nothing of driving a boat, and this can lead to tragic consequences. In September 2008 a man named Michael Cronin was driving his boat on Lake Michigan and slammed into the breakwall near a lighthouse. All 6 of his passengers were ejected from the boat and thrown onto the rocks, and 2 of them, both 9-year-old girls, were critically injured in the crash. Cronin, who was the father of one of the girls, was arrested for operating a motorboat while intoxicated.

Many people also drive snowmobiles after they have been drinking, and that is equally dangerous. In January 2008 a popular Chicago news anchor, Randy Salerno, was riding on a snowmobile that was driven by his childhood friend, Scott Hirschey. Hirschey, who was drunk at the time, missed an entrance to a trail and hit an embankment, which caused the snowmobile to fly 20 feet (6.1m) in the air before it slammed into a tree. Hirschey was thrown from the snowmobile and injured, while Salerno took the full force of the impact and was killed.

Blood-Alcohol Concentration

Law enforcement officers determine whether a person is intoxicated by a measurement known as blood-alcohol concentration (BAC), which is the amount of alcohol in the person's bloodstream. If someone has a BAC of .03 percent, for instance, it means that 100 milliliters of that person's blood contains .03 percent of alcohol. In all 50 U.S. states and the District of Columbia it is a crime to drive any motorized vehicle with a BAC level of .08 percent or higher. Someone's BAC may be determined by a blood or urine test performed at a police station or medical facility or through a breathalyzer test performed at the scene. When a breathalyzer test is given, the suspect blows into a tube attached to the device, and through a chemical reaction it can measure the amount of alcohol that is contained in the person's breath.

> " According to the National Highway Traffic Safety Administration, the word 'accident' has no place in a discussion about drunk driving. "

In an attempt to skew the results of breathalyzers, drunk drivers have been known to do some foolish things. In December 2004 California defense attorney Lawrence Taylor described on his blog an incident involving Dave Zurfluh, a man in Alberta, Canada, who was weaving down the highway and was stopped on suspicion of driving under the influence. After Zurfluh pulled over he tried to run away from the vehicle, but Constable Bill Robinson caught him and put him in the back of the patrol car. Robinson began to hear ripping noises from the backseat, and when he looked he could see that Zurfluh was tearing pieces of his underwear out of his pants and stuffing them in his mouth, in the hope that the cotton fabric would soak up the excess alcohol in his system before he took a breathalyzer test. He ended up being acquitted of all charges because his BAC was not above the legal limit, but whether what he had done affected the reading was considered to be highly doubtful.

The Effects of Alcohol on the Body

Alcohol affects people differently, depending on their physical size, age, health status, and how much food they have eaten. How quickly alcoholic drinks are consumed also makes a difference. For instance, someone who takes an hour to drink a beer, mixed drink, or glass of wine, will be less affected by the alcohol than someone who drinks it faster. Another factor is sex: Men typically have lower BACs than women after drinking the same amount of alcohol even if they are similar in size and weight. According to Brown University's Health Services division, one reason for this is that women have less water in their bodies than do men, which means a man's body has the ability to dilute the alcohol more than a woman's body. Women also have less dehydrogenase, an enzyme that enables the liver to metabolize alcohol, so women's bodies break it down more slowly than men's.

The effects of alcohol are amplified as more of it is consumed. With a BAC of .04 to .05 percent, drinkers tend to feel warm, mellow, and relaxed. As they continue to drink, their BAC rises and other symptoms become apparent, such as a decrease in fine-muscle coordination and impaired hearing and vision. By the time BAC has reached .12 to .15 percent, major impairment of physical and mental faculties is evidenced by confusion, slurred speech, blurred vision, and loss of balance. When BAC climbs higher than that, it can lead to unconsciousness and possibly fatal alcohol poisoning.

Sky-High BAC

In some cases drivers have been caught with BACs that far exceeded .08 percent. This was the case with Meagan Harper of Oregon City, Oregon. In November 2007 a police officer found Harper, who had 3 previous drunk driving convictions and was on probation, passed out in a car in front of a pizza restaurant. She was taken to a hospital where it was determined that her BAC was .55 percent. "You just don't see numbers that high,"[4] remarked emergency room physician Mohamud Daya. Yet one month later, another Oregon woman was found to have an even higher BAC than Harper's. Terri Comer was driving drunk when she ploughed through about 100 feet (30m) of snow and got stuck in a snowdrift. An off-duty sheriff's deputy discovered her car, which was still running, and he could see that she was unconscious. In order to get her out, rescue workers had to break a window. At a local hospital Comer's blood was tested and showed that her BAC was .72 percent—9 times the legal limit. Sheriff Tim Evinger later said that it is rare to see readings higher than .30 percent, and that

> **Men typically have lower BACs than women after drinking the same amount of alcohol even if they are similar in size and weight.**

The wreckage of a school bus (right) and a tree-trimming truck (left) are shown after a crash in West Virginia. Eighteen people were injured in the head-on collision. The driver of the tree-trimming truck was later charged with driving under the influence of alcohol.

levels of .40 to .50 percent are high enough to kill someone.

According to biological psychologist John Brick, the term "lethal dose" is used by scientists to describe the concentration of alcohol that produces death in half of the population, otherwise known as LD:50. He explains:

> Most authorities agree that blood alcohol concentrations in the 0.40–0.50% range meet the requirements for the LD:50. The blood alcohol concentration is the percentage of alcohol in the blood that results after alcohol is absorbed from the stomach into the blood supply. Obviously, studies of lethal dosage cannot be tested empirical-

ly in the laboratory, so the LD:50 for alcohol is estimated from post-mortem cases in which alcohol poisoning was found to be the primary cause of death. However, there are documented cases of fatal overdoses from alcohol at blood alcohol concentrations lower than 0.40%.[5]

With BACs that were higher than .50 percent, both Harper and Comer are extremely fortunate to be alive.

Who Drives Drunk?

A "typical" drunk driver does not exist. People who choose to drink and then get behind the wheel of a vehicle come from all walks of life, ranging from low-income to wealthy, and from world-famous celebrities to unknowns. They are female as well as male and span all ages, races, and religions. Some distinct patterns among drunk drivers have been found, however. Men, for instance, have been shown to drive while intoxicated about twice as often as women, and older people are much less likely to drive drunk than younger drivers. During 2007, according to an August 2008 NHTSA report, 5,161 motor vehicle fatalities involved alcohol-impaired drivers aged 21 to 34, and just 622 involved alcohol-impaired drivers aged 65 and over.

Another consistent—and dangerous—fact is that many drunk drivers are repeat offenders. According to Mothers Against Drunk Driving (MADD), an estimated one-third of all drivers arrested and/or convicted of driving under the influence are repeat offenders, and these drivers are 40 percent more likely to be involved in a fatal crash than those without prior drunk driving arrests or convictions. In September 2008 Uriel Palacios, a repeat offender with 4 previous arrests for driving while intoxicated (DWI), was weaving through traffic in Dallas and was pulled over by police on suspicion of drunk driving. After stopping briefly, Palacios raced away from the officers and ran a red light, slammed into a vehicle and went airborne, then

> **With BACs that were higher than .50 percent, both Harper and Comer are extremely fortunate to be alive.**

These high school students participate in the Every 15 Minutes program, which teaches students about the dangers and consequences of drunk driving. Motor vehicle crashes are the number one cause of death for teenagers. In 2006, 31 percent of teen drivers who were killed had been drinking.

landed on top of a sport-utility vehicle. The SUV was completely crushed. Inside it were German Clouet and his wife, Erika, a couple who had only been married for a month. The newlyweds were killed in the crash.

Teenage Drunk Drivers

Each year more than 6,000 young people aged 15 to 20 are killed in motor vehicle crashes, and it is the leading cause of death for teenagers. Although the number of alcohol-related motor vehicle fatalities has decreased since the 1980s, alcohol still plays a role in a disturbing number of crashes. Many young people choose to drive while impaired, and this results in thousands of needless deaths every year. During an October 2007 press conference, National Transportation Safety Board chairman Mark Rosenker spoke about how serious the problem is. "Motor vehicle crashes remain the leading cause of death for teenagers," he stated, and alcohol remains the leading drug of choice. Nearly one-third of teen traffic deaths are alcohol-related. . . . In 2005, teen drivers (age 15 through 20) made up slightly more than 6 percent of the driving population. But although this population is not allowed to drink, almost 11 percent of alcohol-related fatalities . . . still involved a teen driver with a positive BAC. Countless dead and injured people are the sad testament to underage drinking and driving!" [6]

Adding to the dangers of teenagers mixing driving with alcohol consumption is that they are less likely to wear seat belts. The NHTSA says that 77 percent of the 15- to 20-year-old drivers who were killed in fatal crashes during 2006 were unrestrained.

Drunk Driving Laws

Although the legal BAC limit for driving any vehicle is .08 percent in all U.S. states and the District of Columbia, some states have tougher laws than others. In Georgia, people who are first-offender drunk drivers can lose their driver's licenses for a year, while in Florida, New Hampshire, West Virginia, and Wisconsin, first-offenders can lose their licenses for 6 months. This is in stark contrast to Kentucky, Michigan, Montana, New Jersey, and 5 other states that impose no automatic license suspension whatsoever. Another consideration is open-container laws, which not all states have in place. As of October 2008, in the states of Arkansas, Connecticut, Delaware, Mississippi, Missouri, Virginia, and West Virginia, it was not illegal for either drivers or passengers to have open containers of alcohol in a vehicle.

How Should Drunk Drivers Be Punished?

The most appropriate penalty for drunk driving is often a source of controversy. Some people advocate alcohol rehabilitation coupled with probation and fines, while others say that tougher punishment is in order even for someone who has committed a first offense. When deaths and/ or injuries are involved, it is widely believed that the punishment should be much harsher, such as jail or prison sentences, hefty fines, and permanent loss of the driver's license.

On February 11, 2004, John Templeton received a tough sentence for his role in a drunk driving death—but to him, the crushing guilt he felt was the worst punishment of all. In 2002, when he was a college student in Florida, Templeton spent an evening drinking beer and liquor with his friends at a bar called Club Hedo. He does not remember leaving the club or what time he left, nor does he remember getting behind the wheel of his Ford Explorer. What he does recall vividly is the horror of waking up the next morning in a hospital, lying on a gurney with his wrists shackled to metal bars on the side. Two stern-faced police officers were standing over him, and one said that he was in bad trouble. He had been driving drunk the wrong way on a highway and slammed head-on into a Honda driven by 18-year-old Julie Buckner, who was killed. Templeton began to scream, begging medical personnel to use CPR to bring the girl back, but of course she was already dead. At that point he wished he were dead as well. "I might as well kill myself," he told the officers. "I can't live with myself."[7] At his sentencing, he asked over and over for Buckner's family to forgive him, and because they could tell that he was devastated by what he had done, they asked the judge to be lenient. The judge believed, however, that it was important to send a message to Templeton and others who chose to drive drunk. His sentence was 2 years in prison and 2 years of house arrest, followed by 11 years of probation. He was also sentenced to 1,000 hours of community service speaking to teenagers about the deadly consequences of drinking and driving, was fined $10,000 in restitution, and lost his driver's license permanently. The judge also ordered him to carry a photo of Buckner with him at all times. After serving 10 months, Templeton was released on parole. He was completing his community service commitment and vowed to continue long after his sentence was finished. "I owe that to her and her family," he says. "The damage I've done is beyond repair, but maybe I can make a difference by preventing someone else from doing it."[8]

> **Each year more than 6,000 young people aged 15 to 20 are killed in motor vehicle crashes, and it is the leading cause of death for teenagers.**

Turning Tragedy into Good

A number of people who have paid the terrible price of driving drunk now use their experiences to help keep others from making the same mistake they made, and Tom Melin is one of them. In 1996, when Melin was 26, he got drunk and took off in his brand-new Camaro. He was not far from his destination when he slammed into a telephone pole and hit a mound of dirt, flipping the car over and hitting 3 trees and a house. Melin was ejected from the car and thrown onto the roof of the house. He tumbled off onto the porch and landed on his feet, but he immediately crumpled to the ground, as vertebrae in his back had been crushed and this left him paralyzed from the waist down. In 2007 Melin used his own money to create a film called *Forever Changed*, which is shown to high school students. His hope is that sharing his real-life tragedy will save other young people from suffering the same fate.

Can Drunk Driving Be Stopped?

Although the decline in alcohol-related fatalities since the 1980s is encouraging, thousands of people, many of them teens, still die every year because they either drive drunk or ride with someone who is drunk. In an effort to stop this, law enforcement officials throughout the United States have begun cracking down on drunk drivers, using sobriety checkpoints and harsher sentences for those who are caught. Educational programs in schools, many of which feature speakers who share personal real-life experiences, aim to teach kids about the dangers of climbing behind the wheel of a car if they have been drinking. Organizations such as the NHTSA, MADD, Students Against Destructive Decisions (SADD), and others are dedicated to keeping the public informed about the seriousness of drunk driving by sharing current statistics. Individual

> " Although the decline in alcohol-related fatalities since the 1980s is encouraging, thousands of people, many of them teens, still die every year because they either drive drunk or ride with someone who is drunk. "

states are also doing their part to clamp down on drunk driving by passing tougher laws. In most states even first-offender drunk drivers lose their driver's licenses, and those who commit multiple offenses face permanent loss of their licenses and even forfeiture of their vehicles. In many states people who are convicted of drunk driving are required to install ignition interlocks, which prevent someone with a BAC above a certain level from starting the vehicle.

With these and other deterrents, the number of drunk driving crashes will hopefully continue to decline over the coming years. Yet the real solution lies with people themselves. In spite of the risk, as well as the threat of strict punishment if they are caught, many still make the conscious choice to drink and drive—and by doing so, they are putting their lives, the lives of their passengers, and the lives of others they may encounter on the road, in grave danger.

How Serious a Problem Is Drunk Driving?

> **Impaired driving is the most frequently committed violent crime in the United States.**
>
> — National Highway Traffic Safety Administration.

> **You seldom think of car keys as dangerous—unless they're being poked by a drunk into a car's ignition switch.**
>
> — Bill Mooberry, former executive director of the Naval Safety Center.

On the evening of December 30, 2007, an employee of an Oregon, Ohio, Taco Bell restaurant called 911 to report a customer who smelled of alcohol and was slurring his words. "There's this guy he's driving like a black Ford F 250 . . . and he's really drunk," the caller told dispatchers. "We've got him stopped in our parking lot, in our drive-through right now, and I was just wondering if you could send someone over here to either stop him or pick him up."[9] Police officer Ted Moore responded to the call but by the time he arrived, the man had already driven away.

Drunk after a night at a local bar, 24-year-old Michael Gagnon missed the entrance ramp to northbound I-280, drove above the highway on an overpass, then turned onto the exit ramp heading the wrong way. Panicked drivers swerved to avoid his truck and used their cell phones to call 911 to report him—but within minutes disaster struck. Gagnon, with a blood-alcohol level more than 3 times the legal limit, slammed nearly head-on into a minivan carrying a family of 8 from Maryland. The impact ripped off one side of the van and ejected some of the passengers, while scattering luggage, toys, stuffed animals, wrapping paper, and other remnants of the family's Christmas holiday all over the highway. Five people died as a result of the crash. The mother, Bethany Griffin, and 3 children were killed instantly, and Griffin's baby daughter Vadi was pronounced dead at the hospital. Coroner's investigator Walt Biegala later described the scene as horrific. "I've been doing this for 40 some years with the police department and with the coroner's office," he said, "and this is one of the worst I've seen. It looked like a bomb blast you see in Iraq on the news."[10] Gagnon was arrested, treated for injuries at the hospital, and then taken to jail. During his hearing the following June, he was sentenced to spend 43 years in prison, and he will be in his sixties before he is eligible for parole.

> " The impact ripped off one side of the van and ejected some of the passengers, while scattering luggage, toys, stuffed animals, wrapping paper, and other remnants of the family's Christmas holiday all over the highway. Five people died as a result of the crash. "

A Teen's Tragic Death

Although it happened more than 20 years ago, Jack Blaisdale is still haunted by one particular drunk driving crash. Blaisdale, who was a police officer at the time, received a radio call at 3:00 A.M. about a fiery one-car crash on the interstate. When he arrived at the scene, he could see that the car was fully engulfed in flames and firefighters were attempting to put the fire out. He says that the car was "burning like an open-hearth furnace—so hot that the wheel-wells were glowing cherry red, and fire was rushing out of the interior, making a steady whooshing sound. Bad fire, hot fire."[11] He could hear shouting and was told that it was the

19-year-old driver of the car who was very drunk and belligerent toward paramedics who were trying to help him. Blaisdale also learned some facts about the crash; the driver had been traveling an estimated 117 miles per hour (188kph), lost control of the car, spun around in a circle, and slid along the guard rail. The impact ruptured the gas tank, causing gasoline to spill out and start the fire. He had managed to escape from the car—but his passenger had been trapped inside. Another officer told Blaisdale that because the fire was so hot, rescue workers could only get close enough to tell that there was a body in the car, but they had no idea whether it was a male or female.

> **According to the NHTSA, 16,793 people were killed during 1982 in traffic crashes where one or more drivers had a BAC of .10 percent or higher, compared with 2007 when 12,998 people died in crashes that involved an alcohol-impaired driver—a 39 percent reduction over 3 decades.**

Once the fire was out, Blaisdale approached the vehicle and shined his flashlight inside—and was horrified by what he saw. Only a charred skull was left; nothing more. The fire had burned off the person's flesh. He explains what went through his mind: "'An hour ago you were a human being,' I thought as I stared inside the car. 'Did you have any inkling of this? Any premonition tonight? When you left your home for the last time ever, did you look back that extra second as the door closed on your entire life? The charred skull screamed at me and had no answers.'"[12] Soon another officer arrived at the scene and told Blaisdale that the dead passenger was a female, a 17-year-old high school senior named Kelly. "I was once again struck by an almost dizzying feeling of unreality," he says. "An hour, maybe two hours ago, Kelly was a pretty girl talking to friends on a Saturday night in a parking lot. And now her 'friend' had destroyed her."[13] Blaisdale says that as much time has gone by, he still cannot help thinking about the girl:

> If her life hadn't been snuffed out at such a young age, what might she have become? A mother? A teacher? A

doctor? A scientist? No one will ever know. The fact is, there's nothing ennobling about death. You die, and everything you are, everything you know, everything you ever would have been, dies with you. And before history even blinks, you are as if you never existed at all. Why would anyone risk that to get in the car with a drunk driver? It's something I will never, ever understand.[14]

Varying Statistics

Although every single crash-related death is tragic, there is an encouraging trend: Drunk driving fatalities have steadily decreased since the 1980s. According to the NHTSA, 16,793 people were killed during 1982 in traffic crashes where one or more drivers had a BAC of .10 percent or higher, compared with 2007 when 12,998 people died in crashes that involved an alcohol-impaired driver—a 39 percent reduction over three decades. As promising as that statistic is, however, drunk driving crashes still claim the lives of thousands of people every year.

Yet not everyone agrees about how serious the problem actually is. Although some NHTSA reports compare alcohol-impaired fatalities from year to year, the agency often uses the term "alcohol-related" when report-ing the number of fatal crashes. An alcohol-related crash does not always mean that a driver was drunk at the time of a crash, nor does it necessarily mean that a driver consumed any alcohol whatso-ever. For statistical purposes, the NHTSA defines alcohol-related fatalities as "those that occur in crashes involving at least one driver, pedestrian, or pedalcyclist with a BAC of .01 or above."[15] So, if a sober person volunteers to be the designated driver for friends who have been drinking, and a traffic crash occurs, it is reported as an alcohol-related crash. If a driver who has had just one beer is involved in a fatal crash that he or she did not cause, it is considered an alcohol-related fatality. If a drunk pedestrian walks into the path of a car and is killed, or a drunk

> " The terms 'alcohol-related' and "alcohol-impaired" are often used interchangeably, which can result in erroneous statistics. "

bicyclist slams into the side of a bus and is killed, it is reported as an alcohol-related fatality. This is different from the NHTSA's use of the term "alcohol-impaired" traffic fatalities, which indicates that at least one driver involved in a crash had a BAC of .08 percent or above.

The terms "alcohol-related" and "alcohol-impaired" are often used interchangeably, which can result in erroneous statistics. For instance, a graph on the Web site AlcoholStats.com states that total fatalities in drunk driving crashes have dropped from more than 21,000 in 1982 to 12,998 in 2007, but this claim is not correct. According to NHTSA reports, while 21,832 alcohol-related traffic fatalities occurred in 1982, they included not only drivers who had been drinking but also nonoccupants such as pedestrians and bicyclists.

The Birth of MADD

When discussing the progress that has been made in reducing drunk driving crashes and fatalities, many people give credit to MADD. Originally founded in 1980 by Candace Lightner, a woman from Fair Oaks, California, MADD has seen dramatic growth throughout the years and now has hundreds of branch offices throughout the United States. Yet there was a time when Lightner had no idea that she would ever become the driving force behind one of the most powerful organizations in the United States. The divorced mother of 13-year-old twins Cari and Serena and their younger brother Travis, Lightner enjoyed her life and her job as a real estate agent. Then on May 3, 1980, her happiness was shattered. Upon returning home after a shopping trip, Lightner was met by her ex-husband and her father, who gave her some tragic news. Cari, still dressed in her orange and white uniform after a softball game, had been walking along a bike path on her way to a church carnival when she was struck from behind by a car. The force of the impact knocked her out of her shoes and hurled her through the air, landing her 125 feet (38m) away. The driver, 47-year-old Clarence William Busch, left Cari lying in the road as he drove away from the scene, and a short time later she died. The injuries she sustained had so badly mutilated her body that her vital organs were too damaged to be donated.

As grief-stricken as Lightner was, she became outraged when she learned about Busch's background. After the police caught him and placed him under arrest, they told her that he had been driving drunk, was out on bail from a previous drunk driving hit-and-run crash, and this was his fifth offense in four years. Lightner did her best to remain calm so she could get as much information as possible from the officers. She asked them how much time Busch would likely serve in prison for killing her daughter, and was sickened by the response, as she explains: "One of the officers looked at me, chuckled, and said, 'Lady, you'll be lucky to see jail time much less prison. That's the way the system works.' I felt so helpless. So lost. So angry."[16]

Supercharged by her fierce determination to make Cari's death count for something and to spare other parents the anguish of losing a child, Lightner founded Mothers Against Drunk Driv-

> " In North Dakota . . . alcohol-impaired deaths represented 37 percent of all traffic fatalities in 2005, and by 2007 the number had climbed to 47.7 percent, which was the highest percentage in the United States. "

ers (later changed to Mothers Against Drunk Driving). She joined forces with Cindi Lamb, a woman from the East Coast whose five-and-a-half-month-old daughter Laura had become the country's youngest quadriplegic as the result of a drunk driving crash. Lightner and Lamb held a national press conference in Washington, D.C., on October 1, 1980, and then began to work tirelessly to build their grassroots organization and increase awareness of the seriousness of drunk driving. Hundreds of willing volunteers dedicated their time to the cause, and it was not long before MADD became known as an American success story. Journalist Laurie Davies explains:

> As their fledgling organization grew, they stood toe to toe with politicians who knew the stats but did not act. They took on a powerful industry that put profit over safety. They challenged a society that viewed drinking and driving as acceptable—even laughable. . . . The getting there wasn't easy. It was tough. It was messy. And it was fraught with obstacles. Yet MADD proved, time and time again,

that it would not be bullied or derailed. In fact, MADD blazed a trail that other organizations have since followed. They made hard, cold statistics come to life. They did not just say that drunk driving killed thousands and injured millions. They held up photographs—and described every nuance of their loved ones' lives—to prove it. As a result, a mountain of traffic safety and victims' rights legislation has been passed. Annual alcohol-related traffic fatalities have dropped from an estimated 30,000 in 1980 to fewer than 17,000 today. And, perhaps most important, society no longer views drunk driving as acceptable.[17]

Differences Among States

The nationwide incidence of drunk driving fatalities has declined since the 1980s, but the number rose from 12,945 in 2005 to 12,998 in 2007. Although this is only a slight increase over the 3-year period, some states experienced a much greater spike during that time. In North Dakota, for instance, alcohol-impaired deaths represented 37 percent of all traffic fatalities in 2005, and by 2007 the number had climbed to 47.7 percent, which was the highest percentage in the United States. A similar increase occurred in South Carolina, where alcohol-related traffic fatalities totaled 33 percent in 2005 and 43.4 percent in 2007. Other states that saw increases included Louisiana, Maine, Utah, Virginia, West Virginia, Wisconsin, and Nebraska.

In contrast, some states had decreases in drunk driving–related traffic fatalities between 2005 and 2007. New Hampshire dropped from 32 percent to 26.4 percent, while in South Dakota, deaths dropped from 37 percent to 30.8 percent. Other states where fatalities declined include Arkansas, Florida, and Idaho.

Although statistics are not always interpreted or reported accurately, an analysis of comparable NHTSA reports indicates a significant decline in deaths that involved at least one drunk driver since 1982. Yet despite this progress, the problem is far from solved. The fact is, drunk driving crashes killed nearly 13,000 people in 2007—which amounts to more than 35 deaths per day. Hopefully the downward trend that began in the 1980s will continue, and fewer people will lose their lives in the future because of someone's reckless decision to mix alcohol and driving.

Primary Source Quotes*

How Serious a Problem Is Drunk Driving?

66 **Drunk driving forces parents to bury their children— and children to bury their parents. It strips thriving families of their health and livelihood. It crunches much more than metal—it crushes dreams.** 99

—Laurie Davies, "25 Years of Saving Lives," Driven, Fall 2005. www.madd.org.

Davies is a freelance journalist who writes for Mothers Against Drunk Driving (MADD).

66 **In the United States, where drunk driving is among the most common types of arrest made by police, the number of alcohol-related crash deaths is roughly the same as the number of homicides.** 99

—Michael S. Scott, "Drunk Driving," Problem-Oriented Guides for Police, Community Oriented Policing Services (COPS), February 7, 2006. www.cops.usdoj.gov.

Scott is clinical assistant professor at the University of Wisconsin Law School and the director of COPS.

* Editor's Note: While the definition of a primary source can be narrowly or broadly defined, for the purposes of Compact Research, a primary source consists of: 1) results of original research presented by an organization or researcher; 2) eyewitness accounts of events, personal experience, or work experience; 3) first-person editorials offering pundits' opinions; 4) government officials presenting political plans and/or policies; 5) representatives of organizations presenting testimony or policy.

> **The term 'alcohol-related' doesn't say the fatality was caused by the presence of alcohol. If a drunk guy is walking down the street and a sober driver runs over him while swerving to miss a herd of penguins, that's considered an alcohol-related fatality.**

—Ron DeYoung, "Statistics Indicate MADD's Got It All Backward About Drinking & Driving," *American Chronicle*, February 13, 2007. www.americanchronicle.com.

DeYoung is an editor and writer from Tennessee.

> **Drunk driving isn't something that 'just happens.' We don't spontaneously get inebriated and then 'just happen' to get behind the wheel of a car. Judgment and the lack thereof are reasons for such a disaster.**

—Andre Bermudez, "Drunk Driving Is the New Black," *Gothic Times*, September 4, 2007. www.gothictimesnetwork.com.

Bermudez is a musician and writer from New Jersey.

> **We all know that drinking and driving is deadly. It's dangerous. It's unnecessary.**

—Kaitlyn Coholan, "No Excuse for DUI," *Humber et Cetera*, December 10, 2007. www.humberetc.com.

Coholan is managing editor of the *Humber et Cetera* college newspaper.

> **There is absolutely no reason to think that a drunk driver going five, or even twenty, miles per hour is any more dangerous than, say, eighty-nine-year-old Aunt Jenny, screaming down the highway in her Cadillac at 75 miles per hour.**

—Mark R. Crovelli, "Drunk Driving Laws Cause Drunk Driving Accidents," LewRockwell.com, March 30, 2007.

Crovelli is a graduate student at the University of Colorado, Boulder.

66 **We frequently hear that drunk drivers 'cause 50% of all highway fatalities.' This falls into the category of 'tell a big enough lie long enough and loud enough and people will believe it.'** 99

—National Motorists Association, "What Everyone Should Know About the Drunk Driving Problem,"
November 8, 2007. www.motorists.org.

The National Motorists Association seeks to represent and protect the interests of motorists in North America.

66 **Over the last 10 years, progress in reducing alcohol-related traffic fatalities has generally remained unchanged.** 99

—Michael R. Fields, "Testimony of Honorable Michael R. Fields," October 25, 2007. http://epw.senate.gov.

Fields is a judge with the Harris County Criminal Court in Texas.

66 **Unfortunately, courts and legislatures still regularly cite the inflated 'alcohol-related' number when justifying new laws that chip away at our civil liberties.** 99

—Radley Balko, "Drunk Driving Laws Are Out of Control," Cato Institute, July 27, 2004. www.cato.org.

Balko is journalist whose articles have appeared in *Time* magazine, the *Washington Post*, *Slate*, *Forbes*, the *National Post*, and other publications.

How Serious a Problem Is Drunk Driving?

- The NHTSA reports that over **1.46 million** drivers were arrested in 2006 for driving under the influence of alcohol or narcotics, which is an arrest rate of 1 for every 139 licensed drivers in the United States.

- The rate of alcohol impairment among drivers involved in fatal crashes is **four times higher** at night than during the daytime.

- According to the Substance Abuse and Mental Health Services Administration (SAMHSA), more than **60 percent** of alcohol-related crash deaths among youth occur in rural areas—roads where traffic is not even heavy.

- Michael S. Scott, director of Community Oriented Policing Services (COPS), states that roadside surveys have shown that about **3 percent** of drivers at any particular time are legally impaired.

- In 2007 more than 41,000 people in the United States were killed in traffic crashes, and nearly **13,000** of the deaths involved a driver who was impaired by alcohol.

- The NHTSA states that **teenagers** have a far greater risk of death in alcohol-related traffic crashes than the overall population despite the fact that they are younger than the legal drinking age.

Fatal Crashes Resulting from Drunk Driving

The National Highway Traffic Safety Administration reports that drunk driving fatalities have declined since 1982, but the number of drivers with a blood-alcohol concentration of .08 percent and higher who were involved in fatal crashes has remained relatively stable since 1992.

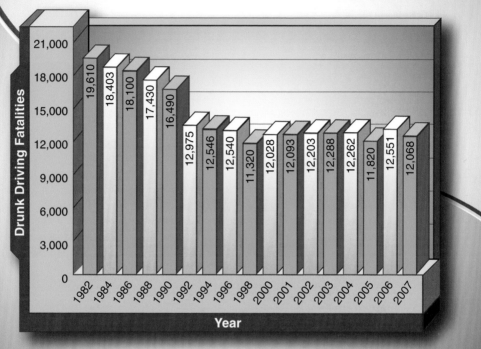

Source: National Highway Traffic Safety Administration, "Statistical Analysis of Alcohol-Related Driving Trends, 1982–2005," May 2008. www.nhtsa.gov; NHTSA, "2007 Traffic Safety Annual Assessment— Alcohol-Impaired Driving Fatalities," August 2008. www.nhtsa.gov.

- The Centers for Disease Control and Prevention (CDC) states that in 2005, **23 percent** of drivers aged 15 to 20 who died in motor vehicle crashes had a BAC of .08 percent or higher.

- In 2007 North Dakota had the highest percentage of alcohol-impaired fatalities (**47.7 percent** of total traffic deaths) compared with Utah, where the percentage was **17.1**.

- In 2007, **1,431 motorcycle drivers** with a BAC of .08 percent or higher were involved in fatal crashes.

Americans' Views on Driving Risks

A survey published in April 2008 by the AAA Foundation for Traffic Safety showed the public's perceptions of the most serious traffic safety problems. Drinking drivers were ranked as the most serious issue.

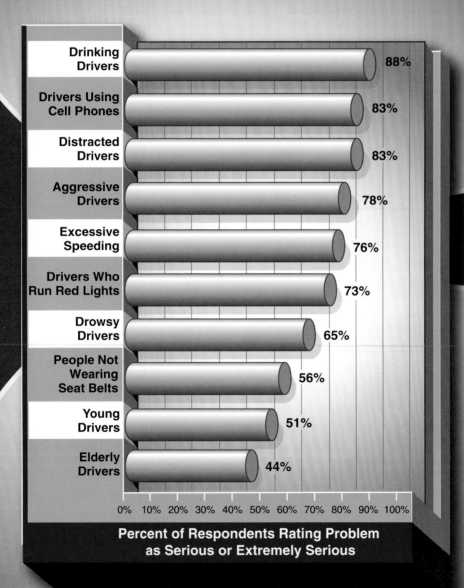

Drinking Drivers	88%
Drivers Using Cell Phones	83%
Distracted Drivers	83%
Aggressive Drivers	78%
Excessive Speeding	76%
Drivers Who Run Red Lights	73%
Drowsy Drivers	65%
People Not Wearing Seat Belts	56%
Young Drivers	51%
Elderly Drivers	44%

0% 10% 20% 30% 40% 50% 60% 70% 80% 90% 100%

**Percent of Respondents Rating Problem
as Serious or Extremely Serious**

Source: AAA Foundation for Traffic Safety, "2008 Traffic Safety Culture Index," April 2008. www.aaafoundation.org.

When Deadly Crashes Happen

Although fatal drunk driving crashes occur at all times of the day and night, statistics clearly show that there are certain times when they are much more common.

Fatal Alcohol-Impaired Crashes by Time of Day/Night—2007

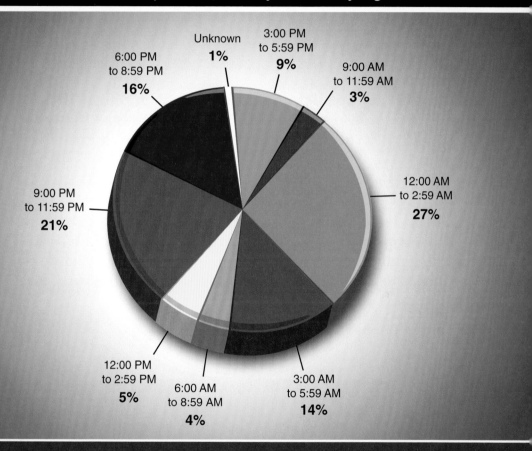

Unknown **1%**

6:00 PM to 8:59 PM **16%**

3:00 PM to 5:59 PM **9%**

9:00 AM to 11:59 AM **3%**

9:00 PM to 11:59 PM **21%**

12:00 AM to 2:59 AM **27%**

12:00 PM to 2:59 PM **5%**

6:00 AM to 8:59 AM **4%**

3:00 AM to 5:59 AM **14%**

- The NHTSA reports that in 2005 more than **50 percent** of the 414 child passengers killed in alcohol-related traffic crashes were riding with the drinking driver.

Who Drives Drunk?

66There is no predictable pattern to who drives drunk and who doesn't. The drunk driver is just as likely to be a highly regarded business executive as a low-class bum.99

—Stan Kid, a lieutenant with the Malverne Police Department in Long Island, New York.

66There isn't really a pattern because drunk drivers are *anyone*. Black, white, brown, male, female, stupid, smart, young, old, the businessman, the girl next door, the housewife, the guy at the grocery store, your friend . . . *you.*99

—Jack Blaisdale, a former police officer from Texas.

All kinds of people, from all walks of life, make the irresponsible choice to drink and drive. Drunk driving is not related to race, religion, or income level, nor is it related to age, sex, or education. Women as well as men have been caught driving while intoxicated, as have teenagers and senior citizens, police officers, firefighters, sports icons, and movie stars. Even respected community leaders have been guilty of the crime.

On August 17, 2008, Carnegie Mellon University professor Jeffrey Hunker was driving drunk through the Squirrel Hill area of Pittsburgh when he drove across a neighbor's yard, ran over a small tree, crashed into a car, and then slammed into a house. He was arrested and taken to jail, where his BAC was determined to be .27 percent. The next day Hunker was arrested again for drunk driving, and this time his BAC was .17 percent. His neighbors were shocked that he was arrested one day and drove drunk again the next, as Kenneth Herz, who lives next door to Hunker, explains: "He has little regard for the well-being of his neighbors or anyone else in the greater community. This is serious. He will do whatever he wants to do."[18] On August 24 the police received a call from Hunker's home saying that he was suicidal, but when officer Daniel Mead responded, Hunker had already driven off in his BMW. Mead caught him and later wrote in his report that he asked Hunker if he had been drinking, and the professor answered yes, he had drunk a pint of vodka. Because he again failed a field sobriety test, he was arrested for driving under the influence—his third arrest for the offense in 8 days. On August 29 Hunker checked into an alcohol rehabilitation facility in Virginia.

Most Likely to Drive Drunk

Even though all types of people have been arrested for drunk driving, statistics show that some individuals are more likely than others to drink and drive. According to the NHTSA, male drivers who are involved in fatal traffic crashes are much more likely than females to be driving while intoxicated. In 2007, for instance, 12,068 drivers with a BAC of .08 percent or higher were involved in fatal traffic crashes. Of those, 83 percent were male and 15 percent were female (sex was unknown in the remaining 2 percent). Commonalities are also found among certain age groups. Impaired drivers aged 21 to 34 were involved in the highest number of traffic crash fatalities during 2007 (44 percent), while those over the age of 65 were involved in the lowest number (3 percent).

Another common factor is that people who have previously been arrested for drunk driving are highly likely to drive drunk again. Michael S. Scott, director of Community Oriented Policing Services (COPS), explains: "By

> **Impaired drivers aged 21 to 34 were involved in the highest number of traffic crash fatalities during 2007 (44 percent), while those over the age of 65 were involved in the lowest number (3 percent).**

most estimates, although repeat drunk drivers comprise a relatively small proportion of the total population of drivers, they are disproportionately responsible for alcohol-related crashes and other problems associated with drunk driving. In fact, anywhere from one-third to three-fourths of drivers arrested for drunk driving have previously been charged with the offense."[19]

Matthew Troell is an example of a repeat offender whose drunk driving record did not keep him off the road. Troell had been arrested for drunk driving on 2 previous occasions when he caused a fatal accident in September 2006. With a BAC that was more than 4 times the legal limit, Troell struck a median, which caused his car to go airborne and then slam into another car that was stopped at a red light. Karen Rosenberg was killed in the crash, and Troell was later sentenced to 30 years in maximum-security prison. After his sentencing, Rosenberg's husband spoke about the loss of his wife: "Make no mistake about it, Matthew Troell is a murderer. The only difference is his weapon of choice was an automobile."[20]

> Spangler had been convicted of drunk driving *7 times* when he again drove drunk on October 22, 2006.

Mark Spangler, a man from Marshall, Wisconsin, has a police record that is even worse than Troell's. Spangler had been convicted of drunk driving *7 times* when he again drove drunk on October 22, 2006. He lost control of his Jeep, crossed the median, and slammed head-on into a minivan that was carrying Scott and Mona Hodkiewicz and their 3 children. Spangler ran away from the scene on foot, and when he was later caught and arrested by police, his BAC was found to be almost 3 times the legal limit. The Hodkiewiczes, both veterinarians, were severely injured in the crash and were unable to work for the next 6 months. At his hearing Spangler was sentenced to 30 years in prison, and Mona Hodkiewicz made a statement in response to the sentence: "Do not let Mark Spangler out, only to crush another father, husband or son to the point of nearly making that man bleed to death in front of his own terrified children, making him endure horrific pain and surgeries too numerous to even count."[21]

Bad Judgment

Studies have shown that many people who drive drunk are well aware that they should not be driving, but they choose to drive anyway. The NHTSA offers a few possible theories about why this occurs:

> Why is it that an individual gets behind the wheel after drinking alcohol or taking drugs? For some, it is the 'I can handle it' attitude. For others, it's that they've done it so often that they don't care, or because they don't think anything will happen, or they don't think they'll get caught. And still for others, it is that they are so out of it that they don't even remember getting into their vehicles in the first place.[22]

A 2008 survey by the AAA Foundation for Traffic Safety revealed that a surprising number of people make the conscious choice to drink and drive. Survey respondents rated drinking drivers as the most serious of all traffic safety issues—but nearly 10 percent of them admitted that they had driven even though they thought their BAC was above the legal limit. "Where's the outrage?" asks AAA Foundation CEO Peter Kissinger. "The [study] makes it clear that while motorists are quick to blame the 'other guy' for deadly practices like drunk . . . driving, too often those pointing the finger are themselves, part of the problem. When almost 10 percent of motorists admit to recently driving after drinking too much alcohol, the problem is much worse than people think."[23]

Carol Reynolds is someone who knew that she should not be driving, but she chose to drive anyway. A certified social worker and family therapist, Reynolds was a respected professional who had many clients. But on April 3, 2002, she made a dreadful error in judgment that she will never forget. Reynolds had spent the day at home drinking vodka. Looking back, she has no idea why she decided to get in her car

> " **Reynolds was arrested at the scene, handcuffed, and taken to the police station where her BAC was found to be .28 percent.** "

and go for a drive, but that is what she did. She was only a few miles from home when she crashed into a car, which was pushed into a minivan and caused the van to roll over, trapping 2 small children inside. Police officers and rescue workers raced to the scene of the crash, and paramedics used the Jaws of Life to get the terrified children out. They were examined at a hospital and determined to be fine, but the older couple in the car that Reynolds hit did not fare so well. The man's arm was broken, and his wife, who suffered from chronic back problems, sustained a neck injury. Reynolds was arrested at the scene, handcuffed, and taken to the police station where her BAC was found to be .28 percent.

> A video camera in the police car captured the look of surprise on the officer's face when he saw that the driver was a young, very intoxicated girl whom he learned was only 11 years old.

She spent the next 24 hours in jail and was bailed out the following day.

Reynolds' hearing took place about 6 months later. She was sentenced to 2 weeks in jail and 3 years' probation and had her driver's license taken away, but that was only the beginning of her nightmare. Because she lived in a small town, everyone heard about what she had done. She went back to work but she noticed that her clients and coworkers treated her differently than they had before. She explains:

> My reputation was destroyed. People were so cold and distant toward me and if they spoke to me at all, there was no warmth in their voices. Finally I couldn't take it anymore so I gave up my job. I started having panic attacks and nightmares, certain that everyone was talking about me and laughing at me behind my back. For the longest time I wouldn't even leave the house, not to go to the grocery store, not to go anywhere except to visit my parole officer, which was required, of course. And those times were especially bad because I sometimes ran into people I had counseled before and I felt humiliated,

ashamed, worthless. When you're a criminal, you're a criminal, and that's exactly how you're treated.[24]

As time passed Reynolds gradually began to feel better, but even today, years after the crash, she is still haunted by the memory of it. "Knowing that my reckless decision could easily have killed someone is horrible," she says. "It's just something I have to live with, but it's still hard. Very hard."[25]

An Unlikely Drunk Driver

Although police officers have arrested all sorts of people on drunk driving charges, every once in a while a particular incident surprises them. One such incident occurred on July 4, 2007, at 10:30 at night, when an officer in Orange Beach, Alabama, spotted a Chevrolet Monte Carlo speeding along a beach highway. He began to follow the car and turned on his flashing lights, but instead of slowing down or stopping, the driver sped up. After a chase that reached speeds of up to 100 miles per hour (161kph) and continued for about 8 miles (13km), the Monte Carlo sideswiped another vehicle and flipped over. The officer ran to the car with his gun drawn, expecting that he would encounter a hostile felon who would try to escape on foot—but when he looked inside, that was not what he found. A video camera in the police car captured the look of surprise on the officer's face when he saw that the driver was a young, very intoxicated girl whom he learned was only 11 years old. After being treated at the hospital for cuts and scrapes, she was charged with speeding, drunk driving, and reckless endangerment, and then sent home with relatives. Her name was never released because of her young age.

"Pattern-Makers"

Police officers encounter drunk drivers nearly every day, and they are the first to say that all kinds of people are found to be guilty: males, females, young, old, rich, poor, and everyone in between. Jack Blaisdale says that it is human nature to want to lump drunk drivers together into a particular category, but it really cannot be done with any degree of accuracy. "What's a drunk driver?" he asks.

> Everyone thinks they know. Humans are pattern-makers; it's a survival skill to have a strong ability to pull a pattern

or information from what appears to be chaotic non-sense. People see patterns everywhere, in clouds, driveway grease spots, in random ripples in the sand at the beach. Humans even tend to classify other people into patterns or "types." Maybe the drunk driving "type" is the spoiled-brat Hollywood kid who nearly kills his friend and gets a reality show out of it. It's the wild-eyed alcoholic trying to follow the white stripe home. It's the teenager carousing and partying and drag racing. True? Sure they are. But these are false patterns, the mind seeing something that isn't there. The only thing drunk drivers have in common, the only "pattern" to them, is that they eventually either end up in jail, disabled for life, or dead. And at the end of the day, recognizing *that* pattern and acting on it really *is* a survival skill."[26]

Primary Source Quotes*

Who Drives Drunk?

❝Drunk driving isn't just the stuff of Hollywood celebrity scandals. It's a pervasive problem throughout the country.❞

—Ted Mink, "The Consequences of Drunk Driving," YourHub, August 7, 2007. http://denver.yourhub.com.

Mink is the sheriff for Jefferson County, Colorado.

❝As in previous years, in 2007, males comprised a majority, about 83 percent, of all alcohol-impaired drivers involved in fatal crashes.❞

—National Highway Traffic Safety Administration, "2007 Traffic Safety Annual Assessment—Alcohol-Impaired Driving Fatalities," *Traffic Safety Facts*, August 2008. www.nhtsa.gov.

Through education programs, research, safety standards, and enforcement activities, the NHTSA seeks to save lives, prevent injuries, and reduce economic costs due to traffic crashes.

* Editor's Note: While the definition of a primary source can be narrowly or broadly defined, for the purposes of Compact Research, a primary source consists of: 1) results of original research presented by an organization or researcher; 2) eyewitness accounts of events, personal experience, or work experience; 3) first-person editorials offering pundits' opinions; 4) government officials presenting political plans and/or policies; 5) representatives of organizations presenting testimony or policy.

Primary Source Quotes

> **❝I want people to know that drunk-driving accidents happen to ordinary people. I was a happy, regular person, and now I'm in prison.❞**

—Nicole LaFreniere, "I Drove Drunk and Killed Three People," *Cosmopolitan*, January 2005.

LaFreniere is a young woman from California who was convicted of a fatal drunk driving crash in 2002.

....

> **❝When people drink, they get a major case of the 'stupids.' It can be the only explanation for why they take such a risk and put us all in danger.❞**

—Dina Campeau, "We're Losing the War Against Drinking and Driving," *Morgan Hill Times*, December 21, 2007. www.morganhilltimes.com.

Campeau is a columnist from Morgan Hill, California.

....

> **❝On the night of Nov. 30 and into the wee hours of Dec. 1, a young fleet sailor had the world by the tail as he partied with friends in Virginia Beach. Now, he's just a name etched on a piece of granite in a local cemetery.❞**

—Ken Testorff, "For Want of a Designated Driver," *Sea & Shore*, Fall 2004. www.safetycenter.navy.mil.

Testorff is with the Naval Safety Center's public affairs division.

....

> **❝I am begging you, all of you, to please not drink and drive. Not only could you hurt yourself, but you could hurt or potentially take the life of someone else and no drink, shot, or beer too many are worth that risk.❞**

—Christiana Sayyah, "Drop the Keys Now—What You May Not Realize About Drunk Driving," Associated Content, February 21, 2007. www.associatedcontent.com.

Sayyah is a woman from Indiana who was arrested and jailed for drunk driving.

....

66 The science tells us that up to 75 percent of drunk drivers continue to drink and drive even when their licenses have been revoked. 99

—Glynn R. Birch, "Statement of Glynn R. Birch," October 25, 2007. www.madd.org.

Birch served as president of Mothers Against Drunk Driving from 2005 to 2008.

66 It's easy to assume that drunk drivers are habitual drinkers, but new research suggests that people who only get drunk occasionally account for almost half of those who drive while intoxicated. 99

—Randy Dotinga, "Alcoholics Not to Blame for All Drunk Driving Cases," *U.S. News & World Report*, April 3, 2008. http://health.usnews.com.

Dotinga is a writer from San Diego.

66 At all levels of blood alcohol concentration (BAC), the risk of involvement in a motor vehicle crash is greater for teens than for older drivers. 99

—Centers for Disease Control and Prevention (CDC), "Teen Drivers: Fact Sheet," July 18, 2008. www.cdc.gov.

The CDC seeks to promote health and quality of life by controlling disease, injury, and disability.

Who Drives Drunk?

- A 2007 study by Johns Hopkins University showed that people who drive drunk are not necessarily problem drinkers, although those who drive with a BAC of **.10 percent** or higher are most likely to have a history of **drinking problems**.

- According to a report by Community Oriented Policing Services, drunk drivers are most likely to be **male, white or Hispanic, between 25 and 44 years old, and unmarried**.

- In 2007 there were 12,068 drivers with a BAC of .08 percent or higher involved in fatal crashes; of those, **83 percent** were male, **15 percent** were female, and the sex of the remaining **2 percent** was unknown.

- The NHTSA reports that during 2007, **5,161** motor vehicle fatalities involved alcohol-impaired drivers aged 21 to 34, and only **622** involved impaired drivers aged 65 and older.

- Repeat offenders are from **one-third to three-fourths** more likely to be involved in fatal motor vehicle crashes than first-time offenders.

- Statistics show that of all drunk driving–related traffic crashes, drunk drivers or their passengers are the most likely to be **killed**.

Drunk Drivers Involved in Fatal Traffic Crashes by Age

Although all types of people, from every possible walk of life, have been arrested for driving drunk, the National Highway Traffic Safety Administration reports that the offense is more common among certain age groups. Drivers aged 21 to 44 make up 64 percent of drivers arrested with a BAC of .08 or higher.

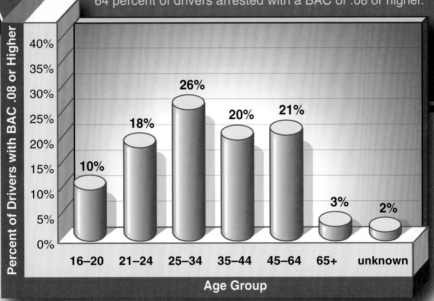

Source: National Highway Traffic Safety Administration, "2007 Traffic Safety Annual Assessment—Alcohol-Impaired Driving Fatalities," August 2008. www.nhtsa.gov.

- A 2006 study by the Pacific Institute for Research and Evaluation showed that drivers with a BAC of .05 to .07 percent are 4 to **10 times** more likely to be involved in a **fatal crash** than drivers who have not been drinking.

- According to the NHTSA, in 2006 the most frequently recorded BAC among drinking drivers involved in fatal crashes was **.16 percent**.

- According to the FBI, of all juveniles arrested for driving under the influence in 2007, **93.1 percent** were white.

Drunk Driving on the Water

Drunk driving laws in the United States apply to all vehicles, not just cars and trucks. Statistics have shown, however, that many people who would not drive drunk on land think nothing of drinking alcohol and then taking a boat out on the water—and this can lead to deadly consequences. This graph shows a breakdown of boating accidents in 2007, as well as the number of deaths in which alcohol was the primary contributing factor. Forty-three percent of boating deaths are alcohol-related.

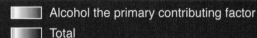

Source: United States Coast Guard, "Recreational Boating Statistics 2007," June 27, 2008. www.uscgboating.org.

- The NHTSA states that in fatal crashes in 2006, the highest percentages of drivers with BAC levels .08 or higher were recorded for drivers **21 to 24 years old.**

Teens at Risk

The Centers for Disease Control and Prevention reports that many young people who do not drive after drinking themselves ride in cars with others who *have* been drinking.

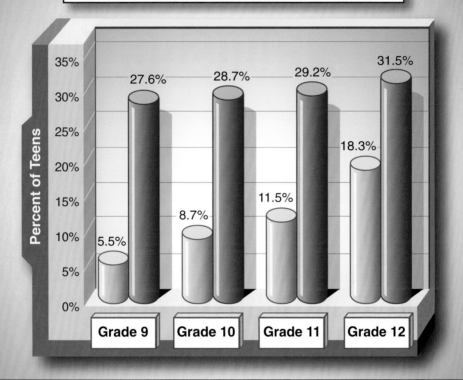

Percent of Teens

- Grade 9: 5.5% / 27.6%
- Grade 10: 8.7% / 28.7%
- Grade 11: 11.5% / 29.2%
- Grade 12: 18.3% / 31.5%

Drove after drinking alcohol

Rode with a driver who had been drinking alcohol

Source: Centers for Disease Control and Prevention, "Youth Risk Behavior Surveillance—United States, 2007," *Morbidity and Mortality Weekly Report*, June 6, 2008. www.cdc.gov.

How Should Drunk Drivers Be Punished?

❝We no longer chuckle at the bumbling drunk who can barely get his key into the ignition—we scorn him. Hopefully, we arrest him, too.❞

—Radley Balko, a nationally published journalist.

❝Although the general public is likely to insist upon punishing drunk drivers—particularly repeat offenders—research suggests that conventional punishments such as fines and incarceration are among the least effective methods of controlling drunk driving.❞

—Michael S. Scott, director of Community Oriented Policing Services (COPS).

People often disagree about the appropriate punishment for drunk driving. Some are convinced that alcohol counseling and rehabilitation are most effective, while others argue that drunk drivers have a reckless disregard for others, willfully committing a violent crime, and should be punished accordingly. Stan Kid, a police lieutenant in Long Island, New York, is one person who strongly believes in the get-tough approach, as he explains: "I have nothing but contempt for people who drive when they are drunk. The pain and suffering they cause is often horrible, and in my opinion they don't deserve any tolerance whatsoever by the courts. . . . The message should be crystal-clear to these people that the risk they pose to society is not acceptable. Their lives should be ruined, just as they have ruined the lives of others."[27]

Probation Versus Prison

During the fall of 2008 Deepika Tandon sent a letter to the superior court in Butte County, California, in which she spoke about the death of her husband, Amit. A popular caterer of Indian food, Amit Tandon had been killed by a drunk driver who was heading in the wrong direction on a highway. The driver, Troy Lee Hovey, had a BAC that was nearly three times the legal limit, and after forcing one car off the road, he slammed head-on into Tandon's catering van. Deepika Tandon was pregnant with the couple's first child, and instead of bearing the pain of facing Hovey in court, she requested that the letter be read to the judge at the hearing. "Troy Hovey is a murderer," she wrote. "He not only murdered my husband, he also murdered my dreams." She asked that the judge impose the maximum prison sentence, adding that Hovey "stole a wonderful man not only from his family, but the entire community."[28]

The judge was moved by the widow's grief and said that his heart went out to her. But since Hovey had no prior criminal record or history of alcohol offenses, and because he was obviously remorseful about what he had done and had a strong desire to overcome his drinking problem, the judge chose to be lenient with him. He sentenced Hovey to 3 years probation and 180 days in jail, with credit for the 60 days he had already served.

Tandon's family, friends, and many others in the community were outraged at the leniency of the ruling. One woman wrote a letter to the editor of the *Chico Enterprise-Record* newspaper saying that she was appalled by the judge's decision:

> A young man who has an admitted alcohol problem drinks himself into a stupor, gets behind the wheel of a car and drives 60–80 miles an hour the wrong way down a busy highway killing an innocent young man and injuring another and he gets a slap on the wrist because the judge knows he has remorse and will never do it again! What does this say about our judicial system and moreover what does this say to society, especially our young people? . . .

This verdict says there are really no consequences for being irresponsible—just do what you want and we (the system) will make it OK. I hope Troy Hovey and Judge Robert Glusman have many sleepless nights over this travesty . . . I will remain appalled for a very long time.[29]

Should Penalties Be Tougher?

Although many people, such as Lieutenant Kid, advocate the toughest possible punishment for drunk drivers, others do not agree that it is an effective deterrent. According to COPS director Michael S. Scott, increasing the severity of penalties does not necessarily stop people from driving drunk because most drunk drivers do not believe they will be caught. Another consideration Scott brings up is that if police officers believe that a potential punishment is unduly harsh, they may be less likely to arrest drunk drivers. Jails and prisons throughout the United States are filled beyond capacity, which means that if more drunk drivers are incarcerated, it would overtax the system even further. He explains: "Using jail resources for drunk drivers becomes more difficult to justify as those resources become scarce. The threat of incarceration, however, is often useful as leverage to compel convicted drunk drivers to accept alternate sanctions such as alcohol treatment, alcohol ignition interlocks, or vehicle forfeiture."[30]

> "Without any warning, a speeding pickup truck ran a red light, roared through the intersection, and slammed into [the family]."

Richard Posner, a well-known judge from Chicago, suggests that punishment should be limited to drunk drivers who cause harm. He writes: "If there are 1.4 million annual arrests for drunk driving, and if we assume realistically that this is only a fraction of the actual incidents of drunk driving, yet only 2,000 innocent people are killed by drunk drivers, then it follows that most drunk driving is harmless. Why then punish it with arrests and severe penalties? Why not just punish those drunk drivers who cause deaths or injuries to non-passengers?"[31] Posner adds that impaired drivers who injure or kill people are already punished, and those punishments are severe:

Why punish the 99+ percent of drunk driving that is harmless . . . ? Punishing just the ones who kill might be more efficient—there wouldn't be as much need for policemen, there would be fewer trials and prison terms, and probably many drunk drivers are quite harmless, for it is unlikely that everyone who drives while drunk has an equal probability of causing an accident. In general, heavy punishment of fewer people is cheaper than light punishment of more people."[32]

Pleading for Justice

When someone's life has been shattered by a drunk driving crash, it is not uncommon for the person to want the driver to suffer because of the suffering he or she has caused. That is how Frank Bingham felt at the hearing of Lawrence Trujillo, a drunk driver who killed Bingham's entire family. In his statement to the judge, Bingham said: "This accident took a couple who had been united as one, and a family that was whole and complete and ripped it apart. . . . An inappropriately light sentence would not only dishonor the three beautiful, innocent people whom we will never see again on this earth, but it would also betray the rule of law that our society relies upon."[33]

Bingham was speaking of a tragic crash that had occurred in Denver on November 10, 2006. He, his wife Rebecca, and their two children, Macie and Garrison, had taken the light rail train to spend the evening downtown. After drinking hot chocolate at their favorite bakery, they left to catch the train back home. The Binghams were pushing Macie and Garrison in a double stroller, and when the light turned green they began to cross the street. Without any warning a speeding pickup truck ran a red light, roared through the intersection, and slammed into them. Rebecca Bingham was tossed into the air, and the stroller was dragged down the street under the truck. Macie and Garrison were killed instantly, their mother later died at the hospital, and Frank Bingham was injured. Trujillo sped away from the scene and was later tracked down and arrested by police. Hours after the crash his BAC was still nearly .23 percent. He admitted that he had been drinking for much of the day, had been intoxicated at the time of the crash, and knew that he was too drunk to drive. He also admitted being aware that he had struck people with his truck.

As Bingham spoke during Trujillo's trial, he explained that the man's reckless actions had robbed him of his family and his dreams. "I am no longer a husband. I am no longer a father. And sometimes I feel as if I am only a shell of what I once was. Despite the many family members and friends who have drawn close to me during this horrifying experience, I mostly feel . . . *alone*."[34] Although Judge Morris Hoffman said it was a difficult decision, he sentenced Trujillo to spend 48 years in state prison.

Are Guilt and Grief Punishment Enough?

When some drunk drivers are arrested, police officers note that they show little or no remorse for what they have done, even if fatalities were involved. They may try to get out of being blamed, become belligerent, or even run away from the scene of the crash, and not accept responsibility for their actions. Others, however, are consumed with guilt and grief. That is how Nicole LaFreniere felt after learning that her reckless decision to drink and drive killed her best friend and two other passengers. "I know that something I did brought pain to a lot of people," she writes. "And I know that the Lord has forgiven me and I have to forgive myself . . . but I don't know if that's possible."[35]

> At the trial, Cook explained to the jury that Daniel had never been in trouble before, and that although he had made a terrible mistake, it was not because of the alcohol.

Shon Cook, a defense attorney from West Michigan, had a client who was also devastated after causing a fatal drunk driving crash. The young man, whom Cook refers to as Daniel, had been partying with three friends and volunteered to drive them home because they were all drunk. Although Daniel had also been drinking, he was the most sober of the group, so it only made sense to him that he would be the one to drive. He was going too fast, drove through a stop sign, and lost control on a gravel road. The car flipped over and then slammed into a tree, and Daniel's best friend was killed in the crash.

At the trial, Cook explained to the jury that Daniel had never been in trouble before, and that although he had made a terrible mistake, it was not because of the alcohol; instead, she said, it was an example of an egregious error in judgment. The jury did not agree, however. They determined that alcohol was the reason for the crash and found Daniel guilty of his friend's death. At that point Cook's job was to attempt to convince the judge that this was a young man whose life was forever changed by what he had done and that his guilt and grief were punishment enough. But the judge sentenced Daniel to spend up to five years in prison. "I always remember that the people I represent—every one of them—are in some way victims,"

> " On a dark country road Neiger-Bickham turned left directly in the path of a fully loaded semi truck. Unable to stop, the truck slammed into the car, crushing it and pushing it several hundred feet beyond the intersection. "

Cook says, "just as those they have allegedly hurt are victims. A case like Daniel's is particularly painful for me, and yes, I do lose sleep over it. It hurts to see such a young man, with his whole life ahead of him, go to prison. I just did not believe that he belonged there and I still don't."[36]

"It Only Takes One Time"

When a person is sentenced to prison for causing a drunk driving crash, his or her family often begs the court for leniency. No matter what the person may have done, it does not change the fact that the family, too, is suffering, nor does it change their loyalty toward someone they love. Many families attend a hearing along with friends and people from the community who vouch for the credibility and reputation of the accused, hoping to convince the judge and/or jury not to impose prison or other harsh penalties. This was not the case with Andrew John Bickham, however. During his son's sentencing in March 2008, Bickham did not plead for a lenient punishment. In spite of his heart-wrenching grief, he stated that his son's 7- to 15-year-prison sentence for causing a fatal drunk driving crash was fair.

On December 12, 2007, 19-year-old Johnathan Neiger-Bickham was at a house party with some of his friends, where they were all drinking beer and vodka and smoking marijuana. At about 11:30 P.M. an intoxicated Neiger-Bickham got behind the wheel of his 1988 Buick, while Terry Ripley, Aaron Pham, and Shawn Huq (Neiger-Bickham's stepbrother) climbed inside. On a dark country road Neiger-Bickham turned left directly in the path of a fully loaded semi truck. Unable to stop, the truck slammed into the car, crushing it and pushing it several hundred feet beyond the intersection. Ripley, Pham, and Huq were all killed, and Neiger-Bickham was injured. It was later determined that his BAC was .20 percent.

> " What people think about a fitting punishment for drunk drivers often varies based on opinion or personal experience. "

At his trial, Pham's grandmother stated directly to Neiger-Bickham that she forgave him, and she asked the judge, on behalf of her family, to send him to a drug and alcohol rehabilitation facility rather than prison. But Judge William C. Marietti gave the young man a much tougher punishment, saying that people need to understand how devastating drunk driving can be. "I've seen this problem of driving intoxicated on literally hundreds of occasions," Marietti said. "What happened here to Johnathan and these boys—up until he took that left turn—is something I see in this courtroom every week. The message just doesn't get through. . . . It only takes one time. It only takes one time."[37]

A Source of Disagreement

What people think about a fitting punishment for drunk drivers often varies based on opinion or personal experience. Some believe that when these drivers' actions cause death or injury, they deserve to have their lives ruined just as they have ruined their victims' lives. Others disagree, saying that long prison sentences do not necessarily solve the problem of drunk driving, and alcohol rehabilitation and counseling are more effective. So what is the answer? How should drunk drivers be punished? Although it is a controversial issue, it is an urgent issue that needs to be resolved—because if it is not, thousands of people will continue to die each year in drunk driving crashes, and millions more will be injured.

How Should Drunk Drivers Be Punished?

❝Penalties for drunk driving should be *much* stricter.❞

—Tyler Cowen, "Paying the Tab," Marginal Revolution, August 16, 2007. www.marginalrevolution.com.

Cowen is an author and economics professor at George Mason University in Fairfax, Virginia.

❝If the solution to drunk driving lies in increasingly severe and heartless punishment of drunk driving, then why is this not reducing the number of people driving drunk?❞

—Mark R. Crovelli, "Thanks to Mothers Against Drunk Driving, I'm a Dangerous Driver," LewRockwell.com, July 5, 2008. www.lewrockwell.com.

Crovelli is a writer from Denver, Colorado.

❝The term 'legal limit' is a myth. A person can be arrested and convicted of DUI after consuming *any* amount of alcohol.❞

—DUI Awareness Initiative, "Important Facts About Impaired Driving," 2008. www.duiawareness.org.

The DUI Awareness Initiative provides education programs about alcohol and drugs.

Bracketed quotes indicate conflicting positions.

* Editor's Note: While the definition of a primary source can be narrowly or broadly defined, for the purposes of Compact Research, a primary source consists of: 1) results of original research presented by an organization or researcher; 2) eyewitness accounts of events, personal experience, or work experience; 3) first-person editorials offering pundits' opinions; 4) government officials presenting political plans and/or policies; 5) representatives of organizations presenting testimony or policy.

Primary Source Quotes

&&I think that no one should be exempt, that anyone, no matter what your status is, no matter how rich you are, or no matter what your job is or how powerful you are, if you get caught drunk driving you should face the consequences and you should be punished.&&

—Arnold Schwarzenegger, "Governor Schwarzenegger Joins Law Enforcement, MADD to Combat Drunk Driving with Special Holiday Season Effort," Office of the Governor: Speeches, December 15, 2005.

Schwarzenegger is the governor of California.

&&We all know drunks who have an amazing ability to drive perfectly after being liquored up. They should be liberated from the force of the law, and only punished if they actually do something wrong.&&

—Llewellyn H. Rockwell Jr., "Legalize Drunk Driving," Ludwig von Mises Institute, October 3, 2006. http://mises.org.

Rockwell is president of the Ludwig von Mises Institute in Auburn, Alabama.

&&Offering repeat drunk driving offenders incentives for not drinking and driving may be a good incentive. Instead of repeatedly punishing them—which doesn't seem to be working right now—perhaps positive reinforcement will help.&&

—Maria Palma, "One Way to Prevent Drunk Driving," SearchWarp, April 7, 2008. http://searchwarp.com.

Palma is a writer from San Diego.

&&Most experts agree that drunk drivers persist in their behavior because these drivers believe that they will not be caught and/or convicted. That perception is based on reality. On average, drinking drivers make 1,000 drinking driving trips before being arrested.&&

—Steve Blackistone, testimony before the Judiciary Committee, Maryland House of Delegates, March 12, 2004. www.ntsb.gov.

Blackistone is with the National Transportation Safety Board.

66 **Sometimes I see representatives of Mothers Against Drunk Driving (MADD) sitting in the courtroom, to keep track to make sure justice is done in alcohol cases. It is their presence and spirit that helps hold these violators accountable.** 99

—Joel Bieber, "Accidents: Drunk Drivers Need to Be Punished," Joel Bieber Firm, January 31, 2006. www.joelbieber.com.

Bieber is a personal injury attorney from Virginia.

66 **When pioneering researcher Dr. Laurence Ross reported that increasing the severity of punishments for drunk driving has only a short-term impact on drunk driving, MADD turned on him with a vengeance usually reserved for drunk drivers themselves.** 99

—David J. Hanson, "Mothers Against Drunk Driving: A Crash Course in MADD," Alcohol Abuse Prevention, 2007. www.alcoholfacts.org.

Hanson is professor emeritus of sociology of the State University of New York at Potsdam.

How Should Drunk Drivers Be Punished?

- **Forty-one states** have enacted laws that offer enhanced penalties for high BAC drivers; the states that have no such laws in place are Alabama, Maryland, Michigan, Mississippi, Missouri, New Jersey, Oregon, Vermont, West Virginia, and Wyoming.

- A 2008 study by the Substance Abuse Policy Research Foundation showed that states with laws that make it illegal for minors to purchase or possess alcohol have seen an **11 percent** drop in alcohol-fueled traffic crashes among teens.

- A survey released in August 2008 by Nationwide Insurance showed that **75 percent** of respondents believe there should be increased penalties for adults who provide alcohol to anyone under the age of 21.

- In four states—New Mexico, Arizona, Louisiana, and Illinois— first-time drunk driving offenders are required to install **ignition interlocks** on their vehicles and drive with the devices for at least a year.

- In every state but Nevada, the punishment for **refusing to take a breathalyzer** test is a suspended driver's license.

- In Arkansas, Connecticut, Delaware, Mississippi, Missouri, Virginia, and West Virginia, it is legal for drivers and/or passengers to have **open containers** of alcohol in a vehicle.

Americans Want Tougher Laws for Repeat Offenders

A Harris Interactive poll that was published in December 2007 showed that Americans are strongly in favor of measures that clamp down on drunk drivers. This graph shows how respondents answered when asked how strongly they supported certain measures regarding drunk driving.

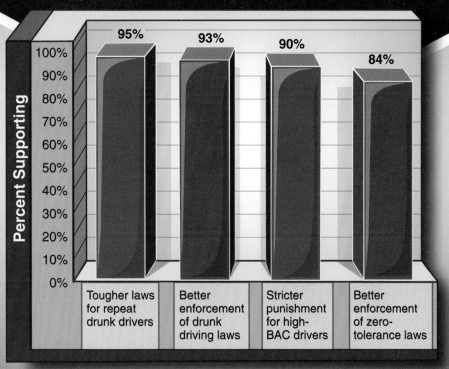

Source: Maria Yarolin, "Anheuser-Busch: Support for Education vs. Restrictions," prepared by Harris Interactive, January 18, 2008. www.alcoholstats.com.

- In Georgia first-time drunk driving offenders lose their driver's licenses for up to a year, while Kentucky, Michigan, Montana, New Jersey, Pennsylvania, Rhode Island, South Carolina, South Dakota, and Tennessee impose **no automatic suspension**.

Many Americans Support Stricter Laws for Underage Drinkers

According to the National Highway Traffic Safety Administration more than 7,300 drivers aged 16 to 20 were involved in fatal traffic crashes in 2006, and 1,392 of them had blood-alcohol levels of .08 percent or higher. A Gallup poll showed that most Americans support tougher penalties for underage drinking.

Should Underage Drinking Laws Be More or Less Strict?

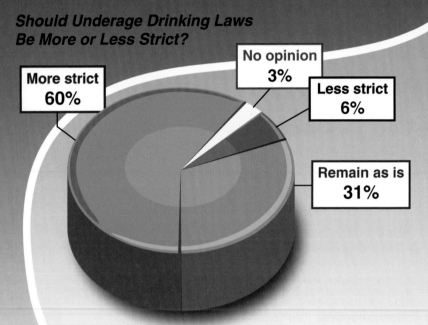

More strict
60%

No opinion
3%

Less strict
6%

Remain as is
31%

Sources: National Highway Traffic Safety Administration, "2007 Traffic Safety Annual Assessment—Alcohol-Impaired Driving Fatalities," August 2008. www.nhtsa.gov; Joseph Carroll, "Most Americans Oppose Lowering Legal Drinking Age to 18 Nation-Wide," Gallup News Service, July 27, 2007. www.gallup.com.

Views on BAC and Driving

Although people often disagree on the appropriate punishment for those who drive drunk, an April 2008 survey by the AAA Foundation for Traffic Safety showed that an overwhelming majority of Americans have strong feelings about certain driving behaviors.

Acceptability of Various Driving Behaviors	1	2	3	4	5
Run a red light on purpose	92%	3%	1%	1%	3%
Drive without a seat belt	87%	3%	3%	2%	5%
Drive 15 mph over the speed limit on a neighborhood street	82%	8%	3%	3%	4%
Allow front seat passengers without a seat belt	82%	6%	5%	2%	5%
Drive with a BAC just a little above the legal limit	**81%**	**6%**	**7%**	**2%**	**4%**
Drive while feeling very sleepy	73%	13%	9%	1%	4%
Drive with a BAC just below the legal limit	**74%**	**11%**	**8%**	**2%**	**5%**
Talk on a cell phone while driving	52%	22%	19%	5%	2%
Allow back seat passengers without a seat belt	60%	12%	17%	5%	6%
Drive 15 mph over the speed limit on a major highway	55%	14%	18%	6%	7%
Speed up to get through a yellow light	45%	23%	22%	5%	5%

Values based on a five-point scale (1=Strongly Oppose, 5=Strongly Support)

Source: AAA Foundation for Traffic Safety, "2008 Traffic Safety Culture Index," April 2008. www.aaafoundaiton.org.

Can Drunk Driving Be Stopped?

66Lives lost. Lives wasted. This has to end.99

—*Milwaukee Journal Sentinel* editorial.

66MADD aims to make drunk driving the public health equivalent of polio. . . . We want to completely eliminate drunk driving at the illegal limit of 0.08 BAC and above.99

—Ericka Espino, executive director of MADD Arizona.

L aw enforcement and traffic safety officials cite a number of factors that have contributed to the decrease in drunk driving fatalities since the 1980s. Credit is often given to the .08 percent BAC legislation in effect in all states, because when the legal BAC was higher, alcohol-related traffic deaths were higher as well. Another change since the 1980s is the minimum drinking age, which has been 21 in every state since 1988. According to the NHTSA, this has had a direct effect on the decrease in teens dying in alcohol-related crashes. Also relevant is that organizations such as MADD have grown larger and more powerful and in the process have helped educate the public about the dangers of driving drunk as well as pressured legislators to pass stricter drunk driving laws. Although there is still much work to be done, traffic safety officials say that these measures have collectively made a positive difference in reducing the number of people killed or injured in alcohol-related traffic crashes.

In an effort to reduce the number of traffic-related deaths, many states have clamped down on drunk drivers by passing tougher legislation. This has been the case in Oregon, where the governor signed House Bills 2895 and 2740 into law in August 2007. Two Oregon women, Marie Armstrong and Jayne Ferlitch, were instrumental in getting the laws passed because they both lost loved ones in drunk driving crashes. Armstrong's 20-year-old son was killed in a drunk driving crash in 1996, and the driver was not tested for alcohol at the hospital. Because of that, the prosecutor had a difficult time proving that he was intoxicated, and he was sentenced to only 90 days in jail. Armstrong wonders, "Is that what my son's

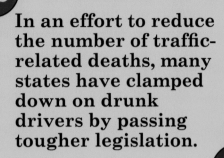

"In an effort to reduce the number of traffic-related deaths, many states have clamped down on drunk drivers by passing tougher legislation."

life was worth?"[38] Now, because HB 2895 is in effect, if hospital personnel suspect that someone who has been involved in an accident was driving drunk they must notify law enforcement, take blood samples, and pass the samples along to police within 72 hours.

Oregon's second piece of legislation, HB 2740, doles out tougher punishments to drunk drivers. The new law states that if drunk drivers who have killed or injured people in the past again drink and drive, and kill or hurt someone else, they face a mandatory 20 years in prison for each person who is involved. Ferlich is particularly pleased with that law because the drunk driver who killed her father-in-law and niece in 1999 had previously been convicted of a deadly crash that killed his wife and best friend. For the second offense he spent 16 years in prison, but under the new law he would have been sentenced to more than 47 years. "Even though [House Bill 2740] won't bring our loved ones back," Ferlich says, "families in the future will have justice for their grief."[39]

States Getting Tough

Like Oregon, many other states are passing tougher laws to fight drunk driving. One way they are doing that is by using technology, such as requiring ignition interlocks to be installed in a vehicle of a convicted drunk driver. These are similar to breathalyzers: Drivers must blow into them every time they start the vehicle, and the device records whether there is any blood-alcohol content. If the measurement is too high (the percentage varies by state), the ignition interlock prevents the vehicle from starting.

As of October 2008, 46 states and the District of Columbia had ignition interlock legislation in place. In most of these states the devices are required only for repeat offenders, but that is not the case in New Mexico. In June 2005 New Mexico became the first state to require that *anyone* who is convicted of driving under the influence, whether it is a first offense or not, must drive with an ignition interlock for a minimum of 12 months. Since that time, Arizona, Louisiana, and Illinois have adopted similar laws for first-time DUI offenders. And Arizona has even tougher laws in place for people they classify as "super-extreme" DUI offenders, or drivers whose BAC is determined to be .20 percent or higher. They are required to spend 45 days in jail and drive with ignition interlocks on their vehicles for at least 2 years.

> " In June 2005 New Mexico became the first state to require that *anyone* who is convicted of driving under the influence, whether it is a first offense or not, must drive with an ignition interlock for a minimum of 12 months. "

Since the new legislation has been in place, the state has seen progress. During 2006 Arizona's alcohol-related traffic fatalities increased 15 percent over 2005, and it had the sixth highest number of alcohol-related traffic deaths in the country. Since September 2007, when Governor Janet Napolitano signed the new drunk driving bill into law, the state has seen a marked decrease in these deaths. In 2006 Arizona had 399 alcohol-impaired driving fatalities, and by 2007 the number had dropped to 336—nearly a 16 percent decrease in a year.

To further reduce drunk driving crashes in Arizona, a sheriff in Phoenix has employed a rather unusual tactic. He has formed a "chain gang" of men serving time for the crime who clean city streets in full view of commuters while wearing bright pink shirts that say "Sheriff D.U.I. Chain Gang" on the back, and "Clean(ing) and Sober" on the front.

Sheriff Joe Arpaio's goal is for the men to serve as a deterrent to potential drunk drivers who see them on the street. "Maybe this will warn people—knock it off, don't drink and drive,"[40] he says. Along with cleaning roadways, another of the group's tasks was to bury, in a cemetery for the indigent, homeless people who had died of alcohol abuse.

States such as Oregon and Arizona, which have made progress since passing stricter drunk driving legislation, can be contrasted with other states that have far more lenient laws. In South Carolina, for instance, impaired driving fatalities totaled 43.4 percent of the total motor vehicle deaths in 2007, up from 33 percent in 2005. The state is often criticized for having lax drunk driving laws, as MADD explains:

> South Carolina—consistently one of the worst states in the nation for drunk driving—has had opportunities over the past three years to fix the loopholes in their drunk driving law, one of the least effective in the nation. However, each year defense attorneys in the South Carolina legislature effectively kill any meaningful reform of their drunk driving law; those obstructions have squandered the potential to save lives.[41]

Should the Legal BAC Be Lowered?

According to the results of a study announced in November 2006 by the Pacific Institute for Research and Evaluation, when all states lowered the legal BAC limit from .10 percent to .08 percent, alcohol-related traffic crashes and injuries dropped by 7 to 8 percent. The study also showed that in countries where the legal limit is .05 percent, including Australia, Finland, and Germany, among others, the result has been even greater reductions in alcohol-related crashes and deaths. One of the authors of the report, James Fell, who has studied impaired driving for 30 years, calls for the United States to follow the lead of other countries and reduce the BAC even more. He explains: "There is clear, strong evidence that lowering the BAC limit is effective. Whether it's lowered from .10 to .08 or from .08 to .05, the number of deaths and injuries from drunk drinking will be reduced and lives will be saved."[42]

What is particularly disturbing, however, is that even though the BAC limit for driving is .08 in all states, the most frequent drunk drivers are those with much higher levels of alcohol in their blood. The NHTSA cites strong evidence that higher BAC levels lead to more alcohol-related traffic crashes and deaths: "A driver with a high BAC of .15 . . . or greater is at least 20 times more likely to be involved in a fatal crash than a sober driver. During an average weekend night, about 1 percent of drivers have BACs of .15 or greater and about two-thirds of fatally injured drinking drivers have BACs of .15 or greater."[43] Because of the increased risk posed by drivers with elevated BAC levels, the NHTSA encourages states to clamp down on these people and penalize even first-time offenders comparably to repeat offenders. The agency cites the state of Minnesota, which has a law in place that levies increased penalties for drivers with high BACs. This has resulted in a reduction in the number of first and repeat offenders with BACs higher than .20 percent.

> " In South Carolina . . . impaired driving fatalities totaled 43.4 percent of the total motor vehicle deaths in 2007, up from 33 percent in 2005. The state is often criticized for having lax drunk driving laws. "

The Shock Factor

Even small amounts of alcohol have been shown to affect young people far more than it affects those who are older. According to the CDC, at all levels of BAC the risk of involvement in a motor vehicle crash is greater for teenagers than older drivers. Because of that, educating teens about the dangers of drinking and driving is a high priority for law enforcement and traffic safety officials.

One educational program, known as *Shattered Dreams*, puts students in the middle of simulated drunk driving crashes, and is intended to shock young people into facing the dire results of mixing alcohol with driving. The presentations are startlingly realistic, with student actors playing the role of drunk drivers as well as those who have "died" or been "injured" in a crash. After the mock crash takes place, sirens scream and lights flash as rescue workers and police arrive at the scene. Those who have supposedly been killed lie still on the ground or on top of cars, and are taken away by a hearse. The injured sit dazed in smashed vehicles or lie on the ground, with mock blood dripping down their faces. They scream in pain while rescue workers attend to them and then whisk them away in ambulances or helicopters. Onlookers, shocked at the horror of the scene, sob over the loss of their classmates and friends. Students playing the role of surviving drunk drivers are handcuffed and taken to the police station. The next day a wrap-up assembly is held featuring the students who played roles in the mock crash, their parents, and participating law enforcement and medical personnel. The presentations often feature speakers who have actually lost loved ones in drunk driving crashes, who want students to get the message not to drink until they are 21 and never to drink and drive.

Another program designed for students is known as *Every 15 Minutes*, whose title is based on the statistic showing the frequency of people in the United States dying in drunk driving–related incidents. During the first day a person who is dressed as the Grim Reaper removes one student from class every 15 minutes. A police officer visits the classroom to read an obituary written by the "dead" student's parents, explaining the circumstances of his or her death and how it has affected them. A few minutes later the student, wearing white face makeup, a coroner's tag, and a black "Every 15 Minutes" T-shirt, returns to the class but does not speak to other students or interact with them for the remainder of the school day. He or she has now become one of the "living dead." In the afternoon, a simulated traffic crash takes place on the school grounds, much like those that are featured in *Shattered Dreams* programs, with graphically realistic injuries, deaths, and drunk driving arrests. The program is concluded with a retreat and a discussion about what the students learned.

> "According to the CDC, at all levels of BAC the risk of involvement in a motor vehicle crash is greater for teenagers than older drivers.

One teenager who was strongly affected by an *Every 15 Minutes* presentation is Hallie McKnight, who attends Loretto High School in Sacramento, California. She initially thought she would not be very affected by it, but afterward she realized how wrong she was. "Each time I saw the Grim Reaper, I started shaking and got goose bumps," she says. "At noon, the student body witnessed a mock crash scene with actual wrecked cars. The graphic and shocking nature of this scene created instant tears in the eyes of many students. I will never forget what I saw on the soccer field that day." Hallie adds that she was haunted by how realistic the participating students' injuries were, and by seeing the apparently lifeless body of one of her classmates being zipped into a body bag by the coroner: "We had to keep reminding ourselves that this wasn't really happening. . . . All of this grief and despair would be for nothing if we hadn't learned a valuable lesson."[44]

What Is the Answer?

The problem of drunk driving has no easy solution. Even with tougher laws, harsher punishments, and widely publicized awareness campaigns, people still make the choice to drink and drive. Knowing the risk, why do they do it? Often it is because they do not think they will get caught. Or, perhaps they are too drunk to realize that they have no business driving. In some cases, these drivers are just too arrogant and reckless to care. Whatever their reasons, if they mix drinking alcohol with driving, they are endangering their own lives, as well as the lives of everyone around them—and their actions have the potential to inflict pain and grief on others that might not heal.

Primary Source Quotes*

Can Drunk Driving Be Stopped?

66 The vast majority of motorists understand that the minor inconvenience of stopping at a sobriety checkpoint, which should take only about as long as stopping at a red light of 30 seconds or less, is an effective way to reduce the risk of a DWI crash or fatality. 99

—Mary Ann Viverette, "Sobriety Checkpoints: An Effective Tool to Reduce DWI Fatalities," *Police Chief*, September 2008. www.policechiefonline.org.

Viverette is chief of police in Gaithersburg, Maryland.

66 To underscore the fact that it is some level of drinking that is being criminalized, government sets up these outrageous, civil-liberties-violating barricades that stop people to check their blood—even when they have done nothing at all. 99

—Llewellyn H. Rockwell Jr., "Legalize Drunk Driving," Ludwig von Mises Institute, October 3, 2006. http://mises.org.

Rockwell is president of the Ludwig von Mises Institute in Auburn, Alabama.

Primary Source Quotes

66 State highway safety offices . . . and others encourage 'no use' of alcohol when driving, yet our society encourages alcohol consumption through the media and our laws permit a certain legal amount of alcohol when driving. 99

—Governors Highway Safety Association, "Statement of the Governors Highway Safety Association (GHSA) for the Oversight Hearing on the Effectiveness of Federal Drunk Driving Programs," October 25, 2007. www.ghsa.org.

The GHSA's mission is to provide leadership and representation for the states to improve traffic safety, influence national policy, and enhance program management.

66 We must stop putting ourselves in positions where we can drive drunk. This means not driving to the bars, not driving to parties, not driving anywhere for the explicit purpose of drinking. 99

—*Iowa State Daily*, "Editorial: Let Two Lost Lives Change Our View of Drunk Driving," February 15, 2006. www.iowastatedaily.com.

Iowa State Daily is an independent, student-run publication of Iowa State University.

66 The purpose of the sobriety checkpoint is to reduce the number of traffic collisions involving intoxicated drivers through enforcement and public awareness. The message is simple 'You Drink & Drive, You Lose.' 99

—Los Angeles Police Department, "LAPD Conducts Sobriety Checkpoint," LAPD Blog, May 19, 2006. http://lapdblog.typepad.com.

The LAPD is the fifth largest law enforcement agency in the United States.

66 The simple fact is that checkpoints are largely wastes of police resources and taxpayer money—not to mention unjustified invasions of privacy. 99

—Lawrence Taylor, "Do DUI Roadblocks Work? (Part II)" DUI Blog, April 20, 2005. www.duiblog.com.

Taylor is a defense attorney from California.

> **❝Founded in 1980, MADD has helped save more than 330,000 lives.❞**

—Amy George, "Miss America and the CarMax Foundation Launch New UMADD Chapter at NC State," Mothers Against Drunk Driving (MADD) news release, October 16, 2006. www.madd.org.

George is MADD's communications manager.

> **❝My favorite example of distorting statistics for self-serving purposes is MADD's own oft-repeated claim: 'Since MADD's founding in 1980, alcohol-related fatalities have decreased 44 percent (from 30,429 to 17,013) and MADD has helped save almost 300,000 lives.' 300,000? Do the math.❞**

—Lawrence Taylor, "Do DUI Roadblocks Work? (Part II)" DUI Blog, April 20, 2005. www.duiblog.com.

Taylor is a defense attorney from California.

> **❝Drunk driving, why is drunk driving even an issue? We have cabs, buses, designated driver programs, but most of all we have common sense. Don't we? Here is a societal problem that is 100% preventable!❞**

—Crystal Sciarini, "How Drunk Driving Changed My Life," Associated Content, February 5, 2007. www.associatedcontent.com.

Sciarini is a woman from Wisconsin whose stepfather was killed by a drunk driver in 1997.

Facts and Illustrations

Can Drunk Driving Be Stopped?

- The NHTSA states that the number of teenage alcohol-related deaths declined after the minimum drinking age was **raised to 21**, which saved an estimated 25,000 lives.

- As of October 2008, 46 states and the District of Columbia had implemented **ignition interlock laws**.

- An August 2008 survey by Nationwide Insurance showed that **78 percent** of respondents support keeping the minimum drinking age at 21.

- According to a study announced in November 2006 by the Pacific Institute for Research and Evaluation, countries that have BAC limits of **.05 percent** or lower experience a lower incidence of alcohol-related traffic crashes and deaths than those with higher BAC limits.

- A study announced in July 2008 by the Substance Abuse Policy Research Foundation showed that **Utah** has implemented the **most aggressive program** in the country to discourage underage drinking and fight alcohol-related driving fatalities among teens.

- In August 2007 U.S. **transportation secretary Mary E. Peters** launched a national drunk driving enforcement campaign and appealed to judges, prosecutors, and parole officers to do everything in their power to keep drunk drivers off the road.

Americans Do Not Want to Lower the Drinking Age

Since the 1980s the number of teens killed in alcohol-related traffic crashes has markedly declined. Many people attribute this progress to the minimum drinking age being 21, which has been in effect in all states since 1988. A Gallup poll conducted during July 2007 showed that the majority of Americans overwhelming opposed the idea of lowering the drinking age to 18.

Public Opinion About the Minimum Drinking Age

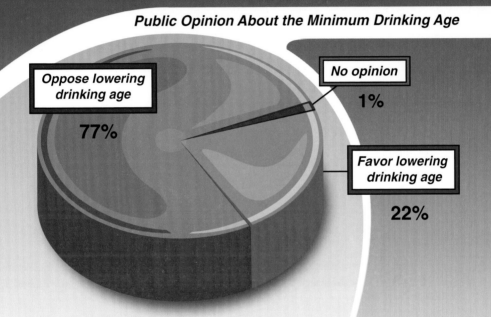

Oppose lowering drinking age
77%

No opinion
1%

Favor lowering drinking age
22%

Source: AAA Foundation for Traffic Safety, "2008 Traffic Safety Culture Index," April 2008. www.aaafoundation.org.

Designated Drivers

Law enforcement and traffic safety officials constantly remind people that if they drink, they should never, ever get behind the wheel of any vehicle. Instead, they should ask someone who is sober to drive them. A survey by Nielsen Media Research showed American views about designated drivers. The majority of respondents thought that using a designated driver was an excellent or good way to reduce drunk driving.

Q: Do you think that promoting the use of designated drivers is an excellent, good, fair, or poor way to help reduce the problem of drunk driving?

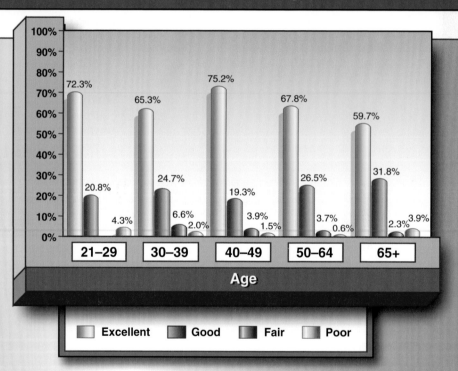

Source: Nielsen Media Research, "Designated Driver Study," December 11, 2007. www.alcoholstats.com.

Support for Preventive Drunk Driving Measures

An April 2008 survey by the AAA Foundation for Traffic Safety showed that the majority of respondents clearly support measures that will prevent people from driving drunk. Sixty-seven percent think people who have been convicted of drunk driving should have testing equipment in their vehicle.

Levels of Support for Various Traffic Safety Measures

	1	2	3	4	5
Requiring drivers who have been convicted of DWI to use equipment that tests them for alcohol before they can start their car	5%	3%	12%	13%	67%
More sobriety checkpoints	8%	4%	15%	14%	59%
Having more police on the road to enforce traffic laws	9%	4%	20%	16%	15%
Requiring all drivers to use equipment that tests them for alcohol before they can start their car	32%	10%	21%	6%	31%

Values based on a five-point scale (1=Strongly Oppose, 5=Strongly Support)

Source: AAA Foundation for Traffic Safety, "2008 Traffic Safety Culture Index," April 2008. www.aaafoundation.org.

Key People and Advocacy Groups

Michael Gagnon: In December 2007 Gagnon, with a BAC of more than 3 times the legal limit, was driving the wrong way on an Ohio freeway when he crashed into a van and killed 5 members of a Maryland family, including 4 children.

Candace Lightner: After her daughter Cari was struck and killed by a repeat drunk driving offender in 1980, Lightner founded Mothers Against Drunk Driving (MADD).

Larry Mahoney: On May 14, 1988, Mahoney was drunk and driving the wrong way on a Kentucky highway when he slammed into a church bus, causing the most catastrophic alcohol-related crash in U.S. history; 24 children and 3 adults were killed, and dozens of others were injured.

Mothers Against Drunk Driving (MADD): Originally known as Mothers Against Drunk Drivers, MADD's mission is to stop drunk driving and to support the victims of drunk drivers.

National Highway Traffic Safety Administration (NHTSA): The NHTSA's mission is to save lives, prevent injuries, and reduce economic costs due to traffic crashes.

Students Against Destructive Decisions (SADD): Formerly known as Students Against Driving Drunk, SADD's mission is to prevent destructive decisions, particularly underage drinking and other drug use, impaired driving, teen violence, teen depression, and suicide.

Lawrence Taylor: A well-known California defense attorney who specializes in DUI cases.

Lawrence Trujillo: In November 2006 Trujillo was driving drunk in downtown Denver when he struck a family crossing the street, killing the mother and two children riding in a stroller.

John Vallejo: A law enforcement officer since 1990, Vallejo has developed numerous education programs to teach others about the dangers of impaired driving and founded the DUI Awareness Initiative.

Chronology

1919
The ratification of the Eighteenth Amendment to the Constitution by Congress marks the beginning of Prohibition, which bans the manufacture and distribution of alcohol in the United States.

1980
After Candace Lightner's 13-year-old daughter Cari is struck and killed by a drunk driver, Lightner founds Mothers Against Drunk Drivers (MADD); the organization's name is later changed to Mothers Against Drunk Driving.

1982
President Ronald Reagan appoints the Presidential Commission on Drunk Driving.

1920   **1950**   **1980**

1933
Alcohol Prohibition legislation is repealed.

1981
Students Against Driving Drunk (SADD) is founded by Robert Anastas, a high school student from Massachusetts.

1966
The National Traffic Safety Board is established by the National Traffic and Motor Vehicle Safety Act; later the organization is renamed the National Highway Traffic Safety Administration (NHTSA).

1984
The National Minimum Drinking Age Act is passed by Congress, which requires that states prohibit the purchase or possession of alcoholic beverages by anyone under age 21 as a condition of receiving federal highway funds.

1985

After disputes with board members over MADD's focus, Candace Lightner leaves the organization that she founded five years before.

2008

The NHTSA releases a report stating that the number of alcohol-impaired driving fatalities declined 3.7 percent from 2006 to 2007; 32 states had decreases in the number of alcohol-impaired driving fatalities in that same period.

1995

The number of alcohol-related traffic fatalities totals 17,274, a 24 percent reduction since 1985.

2005

All states and the District of Columbia have .08 BAC limits or lower.

1985

2008

1988

America's most catastrophic drunk driving crash occurs in Carrollton, Kentucky, when Larry Mahoney, a repeat drunk driving offender, slams into a church bus, killing 24 children and 3 adults.

2000

Congress passes the DOT Appropriations Act, thereby adopting .08 BAC as the national limit for impaired driving. States that do not comply will be penalized by losing federal highway construction funds.

1997

To broaden the scope of its mission, SADD is renamed Students Against Destructive Decisions.

Related Organizations

The Century Council

2345 Crystal Dr., Suite 910

Arlington, VA 22202

phone: (202) 637-0077 • fax: (202) 637-0079

e-mail: info@centurycouncil.org • Web site: www.centurycouncil.org

Funded by the distilled spirits industry, the Century Council's mission is to fight drunk driving and stop underage drinking. Its Web site offers news articles, a collection of facts about underage drinking, drunk driving statistics, and research findings.

DUI Awareness Initiative

PO Box 340804

Tampa, FL 33694

phone: (813) 629-5705

e-mail: infodui@duiawareness.org • Web site: www.duiawareness.org

DUI Awareness Initiative administers educational programs about alcohol- and drug-impaired driving at high schools throughout Florida's Tampa Bay area. Its Web site features a collection of facts, news articles, and a special section for teenagers.

The Marin Institute

24 Belvedere St.

San Rafael, CA 94901

phone: (415) 456-5692 • fax: (415) 456-0491

e-mail: info@marininstitute.org • Web site: www.marininstitute.org

The Marin Institute, which calls itself the "alcohol industry watchdog," is dedicated to fighting what it perceives as the impact of the alcohol industry's negative practices, and protecting the public from them. Its Web site offers news releases, information about the alcohol industry, fact sheets, interviews, and a link to the organization's blog.

Mothers Against Drunk Driving (MADD)

511 E. John Carpenter Fwy., Suite 700

Irving, TX 75062

phone: (214) 744-6233 • toll-free: (800) 438-6233

fax: (972) 869-2206/07

e-mail: info@madd.org • Web site: www.madd.org

MADD's mission is to stop drunk driving and support the victims of drunk drivers. Numerous publications are available on its Web site, including brochures, *MADDvocate* magazine, annual reports, research, and statistics.

National Council on Alcoholism and Drug Dependence (NCADD)

244 E. 58th St., 4th Floor

New York, NY 10022

phone: (212) 269-7797 • fax: (212) 269-7510

e-mail: national@ncadd.org • Web site: www.ncadd.org

NCADD exists to fight the stigma of alcoholism and other drug addictions. Its Web site offers fact sheets, "For Your Information" publications, news releases, and statistics.

National Highway Traffic Safety Administration (NHTSA)

1200 New Jersey Ave. SE

West Building

Washington, DC 20590

phone: (888) 327-4236

Web site: www.nhtsa.gov

Through education programs, research, safety standards, and enforcement activities, the NHTSA seeks to save lives, prevent injuries, and reduce economic costs due to traffic crashes. A wide variety of materials can be accessed through its Web site, including statistics, laws and regulations, studies, reports, and news releases.

National Institute on Alcohol Abuse and Alcoholism (NIAAA)

5635 Fishers Ln., MSC 9304

Bethesda, MD 20892-9304

phone: (301) 443-3860

e-mail: niaaaweb-r@exchange.nih.gov • Web site: www.niaaa.nih.gov

An agency of the National Institutes of Health, the NIAAA is charged with providing leadership in the national effort to reduce alcohol-related problems through research and collaboration with other research institutions and government programs. Its Web site features research documents, news releases, pamphlets, brochures, and NIAAA newsletters.

National Organizations for Youth Safety (NOYS)

7371 Atlas Walk Way #109

Gainesville, VA 20155

phone: (703) 981-0264 • fax: (703) 754-8262

Web site: www.noys.org

NOYS's mission is to promote youth empowerment and leadership by building partnerships that save lives, prevent injuries, and enhance safe and healthy lifestyles among young people. Its Web site offers statistics, research, laws and policies, and reports on issues such as underage drinking and substance abuse.

RADD (formerly Recording Artists, Actors, and Athletes Against Drunk Driving)

4370 Tujunga Ave., Suite 330

Studio City, CA 91604

phone: (818) 752-7799 • fax: (818) 752-7792

Web site: www.radd.org

RADD, which refers to itself as the "entertainment industry's voice for road safety," seeks to save lives and reduce injuries by pairing athletes, celebrities, media partners, and socially conscious sponsors to create positive attitudes about road safety. Its Web site offers statistics, news releases, and a complete list of all its celebrity supporters.

Students Against Destructive Decisions (SADD)

255 Main St.

Marlborough, MA 01752

phone: (877) 723-3462 • fax: (508) 481-5759

e-mail: info@sadd.org • Web site: www.sadd.org

SADD is a peer leadership organization whose mission is to prevent destructive decisions, particularly underage drinking and other drug use among teens, as well as impaired driving, teen violence, teen depression, and suicide. Its Web site offers the *Decisions* newsletter, statistics, numerous publications about a variety of issues, news releases, and a "Teens Today" section that contains news articles of interest to teenagers.

Substance Abuse and Mental Health Services Administration (SAMHSA)

1 Choke Cherry Rd.

Rockville, MD 20857

phone: (301) 443-8956 • toll-free: (877) 726-4727

fax: (240) 221-4292

e-mail: info@samhsa.gov • Web site: www.samhsa.gov

SAMHSA's mission is to build resilience and facilitate recovery for people who have, or are at risk for, mental or substance abuse disorders. Its Web site has a "Browse by Topic" section, as well as a search engine, both of which produce numerous articles and publications.

For Further Research

Books

Dennis A. Bjorklund, *Drunk Driving Laws: Rules of the Road When Crossing State Lines*. Iowa City, IA: Praetorian, 2008.

Joan Esherick, *Dying for Acceptance: A Teen's Guide to Drug- and Alcohol-Related Health Issues*. Philadelphia: Mason Crest, 2005.

Louise I. Gerdes, ed., *Drunk Driving*. Detroit: Greenhaven, 2005.

Jim Pollard, *Teen Issues: Alcohol*. Chicago: Raintree, 2005.

Tamara Thompson, ed., *Drunk Driving*. Detroit: Greenhaven, 2008.

John Vallejo, *Obvious Choice: Alcohol & Drug Impaired Driving Awareness*. Tampa, FL: DUI Awareness Initiative, 2007.

Chris Volkmann and Toren Volkmann, *From Binge to Blackout: A Mother and Son Struggle with Teen Drinking*. New York: New American Library, 2006.

Periodicals

Mary M. Adolph, "Unnecessary Technology," *Cheers*, May 2008.

Mina Azodi, "My Guy Died Driving Drunk," *Cosmopolitan*, June 2008.

Jack P. Calareso, "Keep 21-Year-Old Drinking Age," *Worcester (MA) Telegram & Gazette*, August 26, 2008.

Laura Dean-Mooney, "Carrying the Fight to Drunk Drivers," *Tampa Tribune*, July 3, 2008.

Sue Doyle, "LAPD Traffic Team Is on a Mission—and Has a Message for Drunk Drivers Who Continue to Drive . . . 'Someone Is Watching,'" *Los Angeles Daily News*, August 2, 2008.

Nicole LaFreniere, "I Drove Drunk and Killed Three People," *Cosmopolitan*, January 2005.

Elliott Kleinberg, "Mother Charged in DUI Crash That Killed 18-Year-Old Daughter," *Palm Beach (FL) Post*, August 15, 2008.

Sarah Longwell, "A Sober Look at Drunk Driving Stats," *Tampa Tribune*, June 29, 2008.

Sarah Manners, "Our Beautiful Girl Is Dead, but Her Killer Will Be Out in Just Four Years Time," *Western Mail* (Cardiff, Wales), July 25, 2008.

Dong-Phuong Nguyen, "Driver in Crash Was Drunk," *St. Petersburg (FL) Times*, September 14, 2008.

Catie O'Toole, "Mock Crash, Real Dangers: Students Learn About Threat of Drunken Driving," *Syracuse (NY) Post-Standard*, May 8, 2008.

Emma D. Sapong, "A Message Missed: Why Do Teens Ignore Constant Warnings About Drinking and Driving?" *Buffalo (NY) News*, June 17, 2008.

Karen S. Schneider, "A Sober Note (Richie Sambora)," *People Weekly*, April 14, 2008.

Jac Wilder VerSteeg, "Living Proof of a Dumb Law," *Palm Beach (FL) Post*, August 23, 2008.

Internet Sources

Centers for Disease Control and Prevention, "Teen Drivers: Fact Sheet," July 18, 2008. www.cdc.gov/ncipc/factsheets/teenmvh.htm.

Lisa W. Foderaro, "Police Say 20-Year-Old Stole a Plane and Flew It Drunk," *New York Times*, June 23, 2005. www.nytimes.com/2005/06/23/nyregion/23plane.html.

Jessica Holmberg, "Don't Let Drunk Driving Become a Personal Story," *Fairfield Mirror*, March 24, 2005. www.fairfieldmirror.com/campus_life/1.479364.

Katherine Mangu-Ward, "Scared Sober: Another Way to Waste Taxpayers' Money and Schoolchildren's Time," *Weekly Standard*, August 4, 2008. www.weeklystandard.com/Content/Public/Articles/000/000/015/368amnyz.asp?pg=1.

Dan X. McGraw and Blanca Cantú, "Outrage Follows Deadly Crash Involving Driver with Previous DWI Arrests," *Dallas Morning News*, September 2, 2008. www.dallasnews.com/haredcontent/dws/dn/latestnews/stories/090208dnmetcrash.32a228ca.html.

National Highway Traffic Safety Administration, "Traffic Safety Facts: 2006 Data," March 2008. www-nrd.nhtsa.dot.gov/Pubs/810809. PDF.

Laura Sperling, "The DUI Teen Who Killed My Dad," *Herald Tribune*, September 5, 2008. www.heraldtribune.com/article/20080905/CO LUMNIST/809050309/2127&title=The_DUI_teen_who_killed_ my_dad.

Source Notes

Overview

1. Nicole LaFreniere, "I Drove Drunk and Killed Three People," *Cosmopolitan*, January 2005, p. 106.
2. Quoted in Paul Burgarino, "Parolee's Return Riles 2 Victims' Parents," *Oakland (CA) Tribune*, December 25, 2005. http://findarticles.com.
3. National Highway Traffic Safety Administration, "Impaired Driving Prevention Toolkit," January 2003. www.nhtsa.gov.
4. Quoted in Associated Press, "Oregon Woman Charged with Drunken Driving Tests .55 Percent," *Seattle Times*, September 27, 2007. http://seattletimes.nwsource.com.
5. John Brick, "Alcohol Overdose," Rutgers Center of Alcohol Studies, August 3, 2005. http://alcoholstudies.rutgers.edu.
6. Mark Rosenker, "Remarks of Mark V. Rosenker," press conference, October 9, 2007. www.ntsb.gov.
7. Quoted in Michelle Bearden, "Sobering Decisions," *Tampa Tribune*, November 17, 2005. http://multimedia.tbo.com.
8. Quoted in Bearden, "Sobering Decisions."

How Serious a Problem Is Drunk Driving?

9. Quoted in Meghan Gilbert and Joe Vardon, "Wrong-Way Driver Jailed; Man's Blood-Alcohol Was 3 Times Legal Limit," *Toledo Blade*, January 1, 2008. www.toledoblade.com.
10. Quoted in Gilbert and Vardon, "Wrong-Way Driver Jailed."
11. Jack Blaisdale, interview with author, September 29, 2008.
12. Blaisdale, interview with author.
13. Blaisdale, interview with author.
14. Blaisdale, interview with author.
15. National Highway Traffic Safety Administration, "2006 Traffic Safety Annual Assessment—Alcohol-Related Fatalities," *Traffic Safety Facts*, August 2007. www.nhtsa.gov.
16. Quoted in Mothers Against Drunk Driving, "In Honor of . . . Cari Lightner," May 2007. www.madd.org.
17. Laurie Davies, "25 Years of Saving Lives," *Driven*, Fall 2005. www.madd.org.

Who Drives Drunk?

18. Quoted in Torsten Ove, "CMU Professor Charged with Drunken Driving Three Times in Past Eight Days," *Pittsburgh Post-Gazette*, August 27, 2008. www.post-gazette.com.
19. Michael S. Scott, "Drunk Driving," *Problem-Oriented Guides for Police*, Community Oriented Policing Services (COPS), February 7, 2006. www.cops.usdoj.gov.
20. Quoted in Clara Tuma, "Inside the Mind of a Drunk Driver," KVUE, February 7, 2008. www.kvue.com.
21. Quoted in Channel 3000, "Spangler Sentenced in Hit-and-Run Interstate Crash," October 5, 2007. www.channel3000.com.
22. National Highway Traffic Safety Administration, "Impaired Driving Prevention Toolkit."
23. Quoted in Fairley Mahlum, "Motorists Practice 'Do as I Say, Not as I Do' on America's Roads, According to the AAA Foundation's *2008 Traffic Safety Culture Index*," April 2008. www.aaafoundation.org.
24. Carol Reynolds (not her real name),

interview with author, January 18, 2007.

25. Reynolds, interview with author.

26. Blaisdale, interview with author.

How Should Drunk Drivers Be Punished?

27. Stan Kid, interview with author, September 30, 2008.

28. Quoted in Terry Vau Dell, "Drunken Driver Placed on Probation for Fatal Crash," *Chico (CA) Enterprise-Record*, October 16, 2008. www.chicoer.com.

29. Patricia LaBreacht-Johansen, "Letter: Light Sentence in Fatal Crash Appalling," *Chico (CA) Enterprise-Record*, October 22, 2008. www.orovillemr.com.

30. Scott, "Drunk Driving."

31. Richard Posner, "Drunk Driving—Posner's Comment," The Becker-Posner Blog, December 24, 2006. www.becker-posner-blog.com.

32. Posner, "Drunk Driving—Posner's Comment."

33. Frank Bingham, statement to Judge Morris Hoffman in Denver District Court, October 2, 2007. http://extras.mnginteractive.com.

34. Bingham, statement to Judge Morris Hoffman.

35. LaFreniere, "I Drove Drunk and Killed Three People," p. 106.

36. Shon Cook, interview with author,

October 6, 2008.

37. Quoted in John S. Hausman, "Father Urges Sober Driving at Son's Sentencing," *Muskegon (MI) Chronicle*, March 5, 2008. http://blog.mlive.com.

Can Drunk Driving Be Stopped?

38. Quoted in Drew Mikkelsen, "Strict New Drunk Driving Laws Passed in Honor of Victims," KGW, August 8, 2007. www.kgw.com.

39. Quoted in Mikkelsen, "Strict New Drunk Driving Laws Passed in Honor of Victims."

40. Quoted in Amanda Lee Myers, "DUI Inmates Don Pink in Arizona Chain Gang," Officer.com, July 8, 2008. www.officer.com.

41. Mothers Against Drunk Drivers, "Statement for Attribution to Laura Dean-Mooney, MADD National President on Department of Transportation DUI Fatality Data," August 28, 2008. www.madd.org.

42. Quoted in Doug Toft, "The Case for Lowering Legal BAC Levels Even More," Join Together, November 22, 2006. www.jointogether.org.

43. NHTSA, "High BAC Laws," *Traffic Safety Facts*, January 2008. www.dmv.ne.gov.

44. Hallie McKnight, "Living Every 15 Minutes," *Sacramento Bee*, September 21, 2008. www.sacbee.com.

List of Illustrations

Index

Kissinger, Peter, 39

LaFreniere, Nicole, 10–11, 44, 54
Lamb, Cindi, 27
Lightner, Candace, 26–27
Los Angeles Police Department
    (LAPD), 72

Marietti, William C., 56
McKnight, Hallie, 69–70
Mead, Daniel, 37
Melin, Tom, 20
Milwaukee Journal Sentinel
    (newspaper), 64
minimum drinking age, 64
    lives saved by raising to 21, 74
Mink, Ted, 43
Mooberry, Bill, 22
Moore, Ted, 22
Mothers Against Drunk Driving
    (MADD), 9, 64, 67
    birth of, 26–28
    on prevalence of repeat offenders,
        16
motorcycle drivers, number with high
    BAC involved in fatal crashes, 33

Napolitano, Janet, 66
National Highway Traffic Safety
    Administration (NHTSA), 8, 11,
    22, 25, 64
    on age distribution of drivers in
        alcohol-related fatal crashes, 46
    on age group with highest BAC
        levels in fatal crashes, 48
    on age of drivers with highest BAC
        levels in alcohol-related fatal
        crashes, 48
    on arrest rates for DUI, 32
    on BAC levels and risk of fatal
        crashes, 68
    on deaths in traffic crashes/alcohol-

related, 12
    definition of alcohol-related
        fatalities, 25
    on percent of child passengers
        killed riding with drinking
        driver, 35
    on percent of males involved in
        alcohol-related fatal crashes, 43
    on reasons people choose to drive
        drunk, 39
National Motorists Association, 31
Neiger-Bickham, Johnathan, 55–56

Pacific Institute for Research and
    Evaluation, 47, 74
Palacios, Uriel, 16–17
Palma, Maria, 58
Peters, Mary E., 74
Pham, Aaron, 56
Poe, Ted, 10
Posner, Richard, 52–53
prevention
    educational programs in, 20–21,
        68–70
    levels of support for methods of, 77
        (chart)
    Utah's efforts at, 74

recreational vehicles, alcohol as factor
    in accidents involving, 12, 48
    (chart)
repeat offenders, 8
    likelihood of being involved in fatal
        crashes, 46
    as percent of all drivers arrested for
        DUI, 38
    prevalence of, 16
Reynolds, Carol, 39–41
Ripley, Terry, 56
risks, driving
    public perception of most serious,
        34 (chart)

About the Author

Peggy J. Parks holds a bachelor of science degree from Aquinas College in Grand Rapids, Michigan, where she graduated magna cum laude. She has written more than 70 nonfiction educational books for children and young adults, as well as self-published the cookbook *Welcome Home: Recipes, Memories, and Traditions from the Heart.* Parks lives in Muskegon, Michigan, a town that she says inspires her writing because of its location on the shores of Lake Michigan.